T0041999

Candice Brathwaite is a *Sunday Times* bestselling author. She is a contributing editor at *Grazia* and a presenter on *Lorraine*, and her writing has appeared in the *Guardian*, *Harper's Bazaar*, *Stylist*, *Metro* and *Huffington Post*. She is also the founder of Make Motherhood Diverse – an online initiative that aims to ensure many more mothers see themselves reflected online – and a hugely popular influencer.

Praise for *Sista Sister*

'This book is like the older sibling you wish
you'd had growing up'
Cosmopolitan

'Wise, honest, confronting, beautiful and funny'
Sheerluxe

'Inspiring and provocative'
heat

'[*Sista Sister* is like] that older and wiser friend
you always wish you'd had'
Independent

'Direct, accessible and in parts, very funny'
Guardian

'A sharp, sometimes moving self-help book'
Observer

'A witty, honest and transformative collection of essays'
The Strategist

'Wise, witty'
Evening Standard

'The honest and profound words have been chosen carefully
and speak volumes about society, making this
a must read. Hugely emotive in parts, the author's
warmth and humour radiates off the page'
Woman's Way Magazine

SISTA SISTER

Notes on things I've learned the hard way, so you don't have to

Candice Brathwaite

QUERCUS

First published in Great Britain in 2021 by Quercus Editions Ltd

This paperback published in 2022 by

QUERCUS

Quercus Editions Ltd
Carmelite House
50 Victoria Embankment
London EC4Y 0DZ

An Hachette UK company

A CIP catalogue record for this book is available
from the British Library

PB ISBN 978 1 52941 531 5
Ebook ISBN 978 1 52941 529 2

10 9 8 7 6 5 4 3 2 1

Typeset by CC Book Production
Printed and bound in Great Britain by Clays Ltd, Elcograf S.p.A.

MIX
Paper from
responsible sources
FSC® C104740
FSC
www.fsc.org

Papers used by Quercus are from well-managed forests and other responsible sources.

For Esmé-Olivia, Renae, Sanaa May & Tayah Mya.

You are all 'fifty gallon' young girls,
so never become grown women
who settle for one litre of anything.

May your cups overflow, always.

C x

CONTENTS

Introduction   1

Lesson 1: Snatching Wigs – On Hair   7

Lesson 2: Batty & Bench – On Friendship   49

Lesson 3: Bloodlines – On Family   81

Lesson 4: Tweet, Like, Share, Delete and Repeat –
          On Social Media   85

Lesson 5: Every Mickle Mek Ah Muckle –
          On Money   119

Lesson 6: The Woo-Woo – On Manifestation   159

Lesson 7: The Blacker the Berry – On Colourism   187

Lesson 8: Jungle Fever – On Men   215

Lesson 9: Nine Nights and Forever More –
          On Death   247

Lesson 10: Call Me Cupid – On Self-Love   275

The Most Important Lesson of All   293

Acknowledgements   295

INTRODUCTION

Finally, the time has come.

I've always wanted to write a book in which, when talking about and exploring universal topics like love, finances, social media and more, I'd be able to see myself as the main character. Growing up, I would finger the pages of books advertising themselves as guides for teenagers like me, who were facing a myriad of new experiences, but each one was a hot comb and a tub of blue magic short of being able to connect with me – a black girl fighting against a world that was already making it clear that her position within society wasn't worth discussing. And so, I promised myself that if I ever got the chance, I would create a body of work to try and fix that. I want black girls and women to read my books and to know that first and foremost, I am entering a dialogue with them, because they are my Sistas.

If reading the above has provoked tight knots of displacement in the pit of your stomach, may I invite you to take a moment to analyse why that is. The likelihood is that it's because you feel as though what you're about to read may mean that for once, or maybe the first time ever, you have to sit on the periphery. You are a supporting act rather than the headliner. And I would say, that is very true of what you're about to read. But that's how it be sometimes. Sometimes you have to sit something out. Sometimes allyship is engaging with material where you are an afterthought. Here you get to be a Sister.

Last year, shortly after publishing my first book, *I Am Not Your Baby Mother*, video footage of the murder of George Floyd went viral. Timelines and headlines alike were awash with a universal reckoning. *Finally*, it seemed as though the echo chamber of what black people have to go through was the conversation du jour. Racism – and specifically, the horrific treatment of black people – was all everyone wanted to talk about. There were promises to commit to 'doing the work' and 'passing the mic'. I remained unmoved by most of these ill-thought-out and hurried calls to action. I will remain a pessimist. The low ache which can be found in the very bone marrow of those who happen to be defined as black cannot be empathised with in just a few weeks. This was going to take more time than anyone wanted to admit,

4

least of all those who found that the privilege they hadn't asked for made them feel bad.

And that is where a work like *Sista, Sister* comes in.

Consuming books where you aren't the main character is as important as filling up your online shopping cart with books by black authors in the time we've got before the next murder of another unarmed black man – because there will be another one – goes viral. But only connecting with the work of black authors just to try and erase a sense of guilt you may consciously or subconsciously tussle with isn't the best way to educate yourself. You must get comfortable with continuously feeling uncomfortable, with asking respectful questions, with engaging with material by black people – not only in times of trauma but in times of triumph too.

I understand that my readership is broad, but it would be performative of me to act as though *Sista, Sister* has been written with the universal experience of womanhood in mind. I, as one woman, irrespective of the box I tick on the census form, would fail catastrophically at trying to be everything to everyone. There will, of course, be times when the subject matter has clear intersections, and a variety of people will be able to connect with it, but it is of utmost importance to me that I am able to fulfil that promise I made for myself.

Knowing who I was talking to didn't make bringing this collection of essays together any easier, though. Crafting this was a struggle.

My head aches at having had to reach back into my memory bank to find the words you will be reading. Many of the conflicts were fought by a woman much younger than the one who now sits at this laptop. Several of the stories would make me flush crimson if not for the wonderful camouflage that my melanin provides. But if my sporadic embarrassment means that people feel less alone, or able to imagine themselves coming out of the other end of a difficult situation, then it's worth it. This book is broken down into ten life lessons I've learned the hard way. I hope by sharing some of my insights, the road you travel on won't be as rocky for you.

Let's do this.

Lesson 1

SNATCHING WIGS – ON HAIR

As I sit down to write, I feel a heaviness in my arms. I could put it down to the brutal gym session I did this morning, but I think it's far more likely to do with the activity of the last four hours. You see, I'm unpicking my daughter's locs at the moment, all one hundred and two of them. This is a painstaking process that I started a few days ago, and yet is only just beginning; it's going to take us weeks to complete. At first it took me almost an hour to unpick one loc, but after many late-night YouTube sessions, I found ways to make the process a little easier, and I am proud to share that I can now unpick three within the same time frame.

With every session, my daughter replicates a seated position that so many black women, including myself, have taken before her – cross-legged between my legs – and as I apply water and conditioner over and over again to her locs, I can't help but use the time it's taking to meditate on what hair means to me, to her, to us.

Of all the relationships we black women undertake, I have to say I think none is more complicated, fulfilling, overwhelming, time-consuming and financially draining as the one we have with our hair. And I can say that with confidence, because I have lived it.

If I think back far enough, I can still remember the soft shimmer of joy I felt when I was allowed to choose my own hair accessories. This treat was usually reserved for when my grandparents took me on our annual trip to visit extended family in New York City. One particular shopping expedition stands out. I must have been about six or seven years old. Walking down Flatbush Avenue, the pull of the local hair shops would be too much for my nan and great aunt to ignore and so into each one we would tumble, convinced that this treasure trove of an enclave would have more goodies than the one before it.

In each shop, I would choose the biggest, brightest hair bobbles my young, wide eyes could spot. Maybe some beads, and definitely some of those sorbet-coloured clips that reminded you which day of the week it was, just in case you had forgotten. Stepping back onto the sidewalk, my smile was as bright as the sun, which was so hot it seemed determined to set the city on fire. Later that evening, I incessantly bugged my older cousins – those I knew were good at canerowing (and yes, I know both the judge and jury are still out on whether it's canerows or cornrows, but I prefer the former) – to change my hairstyle.

One of my cousins, Veronica, weaved those strands like an artist. Criss-crosses, zigzags, overlaps – you name it, she did it. Her reputation for being the best of the best caught the attention of teenage girls from 'around the way' who wanted to get fly for one reason or another. If I was quiet and made myself small, sometimes Veronica would allow me in her bedroom, which sat at the very top of the brownstone in which my aunt lived.

That bedroom was more of a beauty parlour than anything else. It was full of make-up and there was hair paraphernalia everywhere. She even had a set of iron hair tongs, the ceramic ones that had what looked like their own oven, and a stand-up hooded dryer (although it was usually camouflaged by clothes). I would make a space for myself on the bed as Veronica worked on her friends' hair and listen to them talk about their studies, boys and how much they hated their part-time jobs. I don't know if it was the smell of so many hair products, or the up-and-down inflections of their Brooklyn accents, but either way I would always have to fight sleep so I could witness the grand reveal at the end. Veronica would spin the swivel chair back and forth, holding one of those five-dollar mirrors that had a long handle.

'Girl, look at you. You look so bomb,' she would coo, smiling at both the image before her and her handiwork.

'Yeah, hunny, you did that, Vee,' they would respond, as Veronica covered their faces and finished the look with some oil sheen. And I would finally drift off on a soothing wave of sleep to the soft hum of TLC singing about waterfalls.

That was my first understanding of just how transformative hair could be for black girls. All of these young women of course had completely different personalities, but the one thing they all had in common was that when they arrived, their tone and body language would be reserved, as if they were tortoises who didn't want to come out of their shell. But by the time the residue of that oil sheen had settled, it was like they had become *Vogue* cover girls. All of a sudden, their eyes were as wide as saucers, their shoulders were thrown back and their hearts were open. Veronica had not only given them a new hairstyle, she had also given them a new level of confidence.

Now that I'm older and able to identify the many nuances and layers to these sessions, I also understand how much more than a hairstylist Veronica was: she was a friend; a therapist; a stylist; hell, sometimes even a teacher. It became clear very early on that having your hair done wasn't just about the hairstyle. That was the least important element of the ritual. It was about identity.

Finally, on that same trip, it was my turn to sit at Veronica's altar. After my trip to the hair shops, I had decided my time had come, much to Veronica's reluctance.

'Candice, I want to, but I know you're going to moan, and I don't want to hear the whining. It's too hot to be too bothered and I've got someone coming in a few hours,' she warned.

'I promise I won't, I promise,' I pleaded, holding my plastic bag of new hair accessories aloft as if it were a bribe.

It didn't take long to break her down.

'OK, OK,' she relented. 'Go and find a comb and some Sulfur8.'

Urgh, the blasted Sulfur8. I hated the smell, but in this moment the knowledge it would make me heave wasn't as strong as my desire to have a new hairstyle. I couldn't believe I'd finally get to look in that mirror and experience what the other older girls had felt.

Just like Esmé was doing so many years later, I sat cross-legged and nestled between her legs. I had the Sulfur8 in one hand and my bag of gems in the other. The reality was, I hated having my hair done. My hair was coarse and thick. Years later I would come to find out that the technical name or code for my hair type is 4C, but there was no internet back then; all I knew is that some days my shit broke combs. And it hurt. With every part and pull, I would wince and wiggle until, in true black mother archetype fashion, whoever was doing my hair would hold the comb menacingly aloft and ask me if I would indeed like something to cry for. Most times, my tear ducts could suck that water right back up with Flo-Jo-type speed, but on some occasions, I would just keep crying. Within seconds I would feel the sting of the comb on the back of my neck and on my ears.

'Stop the noise! I'm trying to help you. You need to understand that pain is beauty!' would be the common retort.

So, by the time Veronica was pulling my head to and fro, I had learned to bite my tongue and fight the pain. Plus, I didn't want her to get so mad that she would just up and leave me with half a head done; no pain was equal to the embarrassment of an unfinished hairstyle.

An hour or so later, she told me to cover my eyes as she bedazzled my now finished look with the oil sheen.

'Almost done. But first, open the bag for me,' she ordered.

So much time had passed, I had almost forgotten about my new hair clips and bobbles. She put the finishing touches to my hair with my accessories. I waited patiently for my moment.

'Come here so you can look in the mirror,' Veronica instructed.

I looked. I couldn't believe it. I resembled one of those black girls on the packaging of hair products. I jumped up and down, squealing.

'Thank you, Auntie Veronica!' I yelled, throwing myself on her. Yes, she was my cousin, but she was older than me and where I'm from that means you need to put Auntie or Uncle in front of that person's name.

'Oh, that's no problem. You look like such a cutie. Just promise me that you will never ever perm your hair, OK? That relaxer stuff is too bad for it.'

'OK!' I hastily promised as I bounded down the stairs to show everyone my new 'do.

Almost a decade later, as I sat in the hairdresser's and felt the premature prickles of what could soon turn into a severe burn start to radiate through my scalp, Auntie Veronica's plea popped back into my head. Quickly, I shoved the memory away; now was not the time. I had wasted a lot of energy trying to get my 4C hair to bend to my ungodly will, but no matter how much I tried to get it to drop towards the floor, it seemed intent on growing towards heaven. Whilst I wish I'd remembered the promise I'd thoughtlessly made to Veronica all that time ago, things had changed the moment I started secondary school. That's when it became apparent that your hair, its texture and the way it could be styled was a status symbol. Any wisdom Veronica had tried to pass on to me had flown right out of my head.

At school there was one girl whose hair really stood out.

She was much older than me, as I was in my second year when she was starting her last year. Jade was her name. Lighter-skinned and with long silky 'coolie' hair, she would wear her backside-grazing tresses in a 'fan' high atop her head. The baby hairs at the front would be artfully manoeuvred into soft swirls and squiggles that framed her face in such a beautiful way. Everyone wanted hair like Jade. Jade had what the black community call 'good hair'. Good hair doesn't shrink; good hair grows down not up; good hair is kink-free enough so that painful post-wash detangling is not an issue, but has enough density so that braids will last at least two weeks.

I was reminded of the fact that my hair was the opposite of good hair at every turn – especially by Lauren, a girl in my class, who was a wizard at canerows. She was so good that she had a great business going by charging us, her classmates, a fiver for half a head. I would save my dinner money to be able to have my hair done by Lauren, even if I knew it would come with a large side serving of embarrassment as she kept a running commentary about what my unfortunate genes had gifted me. Whilst Lauren didn't have hair like Jade's, hers too could be defined as good, as it had a looser kink which made it easier to manage.

'Urgh, Candice, your hair is so nappy, man, I should charge you extra,' she would bellow so the whole school courtyard could hear her. She'd go on to warn me, 'Sooner or later you're going to have to drop a lick of perm in this. If I'm struggling like this, a proper hairstylist won't want to touch it.'

'You know my mum isn't going to let me perm my hair, Lauren, you know this,' I sighed.

And it was true. Even though my mother herself had flirted with every hairstyle under the sun and I'd go with her to watch her hair get retouched at June's salon, she was strict about not allowing me to perm mine.

June's salon was just off Brixton Hill and, no matter the season, the windows would be steamy due to all the hair-styling tools and products being used in tandem. Even though finding a spare seat at June's was harder than finding a sixty-pound note, I loved the atmosphere because it reminded me of being in Veronica's bedroom. The only difference was the women were not teenagers with fickle dating problems or teachers they couldn't stand, but grown women recounting how they found out their husband was cheating on them and how they were planning to set fire to his car, *Waiting to Exhale* style. I also liked June because she was always telling me how much she loved my hair and skin.

'Candice, what are you reading today? Because I know you're always reading,' she would say, chuckling. I would show her my latest book before she would remind me that I was beautiful as I am.

'Now, don't watch what these women are doing in here, yuh hear? Your hair is perfect as it is. No need for chemicals or attachments.'

I would nod before turning my eyes back to my book whilst keeping my ears open so I could eavesdrop on all that fascinating and unfiltered adult conversation. I found comfort in June's shop and in her words. As I grew up, I would learn to understand that she was right; it wasn't just the desire for Kanekalon – a fibre used for braiding more elaborate canerows – my biggest fight would be against the pull of chemically processing hair. A task which is more commonly referred to as perming, although not to be confused with how white women permed their hair in the eighties. Where I came from the most common slang for perm was creamy crack. But it wouldn't be that alone I would have to try and not become addicted to – it was also the feeling that I should be investing in wigs and weaves.

Hair wigs and extensions are a billion-dollar business. PR Newswire reported that it would reach revenues of more than ten billion, in fact, by 2023. That's a lot of bucks for bundles (that's the nickname given to this commodity, because a collection of synthetic or human hair is sold by the bundle). Black women have supported the hair industry's growth to an eye-watering level. There is data which claims that black British women spend almost six times more on their haircare than their white counterparts. Social media is populated with weave sellers offering you the best price on bundles, frontals and closures. There is a huge number of black women who are so highly self-educated when it comes to all things to do with hair and hair styling, and it pleases me to see many young black women quite literally taking matters into their own hands and becoming owners of small hair businesses. But I'm still amazed that more hair shops which primarily sell products and hair (both human and synthetic) with black women as their target market aren't exclusively black-owned. Especially when most of these hair shops are owned by people who are usually from backgrounds that are very anti-black. So much so that products which are used quite literally to strip the skin of any of its deep hue – more commonly referred to as bleaching creams – are always positioned front and centre (but more on that later on).

I was twelve when I got my first set of extensions. They were single plaits that came down just below my shoulders, and they took five packets of Kanekalon to achieve. Back then Kanekalon was mockingly referred to as 'horse hair' because it had the same texture as a horse's mane and tail, but in reality it was just synthetic, fake hair made by spinning man-made ingredients together. The other option was human hair, which is now usually sourced in Malaysia or Brazil. But back then, the only kind available was Indian and I couldn't tell you much about that, other than that I couldn't afford it. The artificial stuff cost one pound per pack, so at least that meant I would have change to grab a Supermalt and saltfish pattie should I get hungry.

Of course, the hairstylists were never happy about using synthetic hair. It was rough to the touch and tangled easily, adding even more time onto what was often a standard six-hour process.

One thing I noticed very early on in the journey with my hair is that the hairstyle you'd end up with usually depended on where the hairdresser was from. West African hairstylists seemed to have knitting needles for fingers. Their talent for grabbing half an inch of hair and forcing it to stay attached to a braid or lie flat in rows was unmatched. But if you were looking for styles for relaxed hair, be that a bomb set of finger waves, a scraped-back pony or a full head of weave, Jamaican hairstylists were your go-to. With a tub of pink styler gel, a tail comb and a set of tongs, there was nothing they couldn't achieve. Whilst I preferred the laid-back vibe of the latter, I didn't have relaxed hair, so I had to face the tug of war with West African braiders.

And, just to be clear, this wasn't any type of pampering session. You too were put to work. It would be my job to keep hold of the ponytail of false hair, ensure it didn't get tangled, whilst also providing the stylist with exactly the right number of strands needed for the next braid. Of course, they never told you how much they actually needed; you would just hear the kissing of teeth and a few exasperated sighs if you happened to provide too much or too little.

Much like how June's salon was back in the day, this particular salon was always so busy that most hairstylists didn't stop for lunch. They were always grazing on essential snacks, and no matter the time of day or year, you could bet your last pound on the fact that there would be at least three rogue children running around who didn't seem to belong to anyone in particular. I was always transfixed by the ladies who carried their babies in brightly coloured Ankara cloth. They would move like ballerinas, unencumbered by the weight of their child, who was almost always in la la land. As the sky would turn from cerulean to sand and then inevitably to violet, all of a sudden more hands would descend on my head to ensure that the braids could be finished before the rattling shutters descended over the front door.

That's when, after listening to hours of punctuated passionate and opinionated conversation I couldn't quite follow, I would hear the magic instruction: 'Someone put the kettle on!'

Immediately my shoulders relaxed. I remembered watching this part of the process when my mother was getting her backside-grazing twists put in. They needed piping hot water to seal the ends of the braids, so they would boil a kettle and then pour that piping hot water into a bowl before dip, dip, dipping the hair and quickly wrapping the braids in a towel so the client didn't get third-degree burns on their back. By now I couldn't tell what was in more pain, my arse or my head. The two paracetamol my mother and friends had told me to take in anticipation of having what felt like a Range Rover parked on my skull had long since worn off.

Yet my head was made lighter with the anticipation of how I'd look like at the end. I was going for Lauryn Hill in her role as Rita in *Sister Act 2*. She had her braids bunched up into a ponytail at the top of her head, and they cascaded down around her face in a way that looked really stylish. I can still remember the first time I saw that movie. My nan had it on VHS and I watched it so many times, I knew it line by line. I especially connected with the character of Rita. Sure, I wasn't yet a moody teenager, but seeing the richness of her skin and fullness of her lips gave me great comfort. Apart from the American sitcom *Moesha*, I rarely saw girls who looked like me on-screen. The image of Rita with her nonchalance, sass and single-plait braids was always something that gave me comfort in my looks. At last, my time had come to look like her, now that I was finally allowed to get extensions. As times have changed, it's more common to see younger black girls having extensions put into their hair. But when I was younger, extensions and perms wouldn't even be considered until you reached secondary school, and now I understand that it's because the detrimental effects of both are very real. If your braids are too tight or your perm is left in too long, you could lose the hair from your scalp forever, and that's no fun for anyone. But in this moment, I finally felt I had arrived.

I had been able to peek at my hair only a handful of times during the process. Between the heaving backsides of the aunties, the general busyness of the salon and me feeling too young to ask to see how things were going, the entire process felt like an episode of *Stars in Their Eyes*. So, by the time the dipping in the boiling water was over, I was a bundle of nerves.

'OK, you can stand up now,' one of the ladies ordered.

This was it; this was my walking-through-the-mist moment. Slowly, I let my eyes lock onto my reflection. I squinted. This can't be right, I thought. I took my glasses off, cleaned them, put them on and looked again. I didn't look like Rita at all. In fact, I thought I looked like one of those dolls that instead of hair had Play-Doh growing out of its head.

'It's good. It's good,' the main auntie of the shop said to me.

I wanted so badly to disagree, but I knew better than to

do so, as it would definitely be taken as me disrespecting my elders, and no doubt that would reach back to my mother. And I wasn't in the mood for being told off by everyone in the family, including those overseas, who would undoubtedly be told about the incident. Instead, I painted a false smile on my face, begrudgingly parted with fifty pounds, and cried all the way home.

That was the beginning of what would be many more false starts and failures with my hair. I have lost count how many times I repeatedly asked if they could do the Beyoncé 'Check On It' canerows – you know, like the ones she wears in that video – only for me to leave the salon broken-hearted. By the time I was finally allowed to relax my hair, I was so overjoyed at the possibility of it being tame and straight enough for me to manage by myself that the warnings from others who had felt the (quite literal) burn of relaxers were falling on deaf ears. This would be different for me; I was sure of it.

'Now, why would you let her perm her good, thick hair?' I heard my nan asking my mother. 'There is nothing that a good old hot comb can't fix. And then you only need to wet it to get it back to normal. All perm does is eat out your head. This is a bad idea,' she warned.

I heard the sound of my mother dragging on her cigarette.

'She's in secondary school now. What do you want her to do? She's surrounded by girls who get to experiment with their hair. Also, all of these hairstyles are costing a fortune.'

You tell her, I thought. The last time my nan had hot-combed my hair she had burned us both and my hair in the process. And then the bloody hairstyle had barely lasted forty-eight hours. I needed something a little more permanent.

Later that week after school, I stopped at the hair shop again. They knew me well now.

'No Kanekalon today?' the copper-toned man laughed as I approached the till.

'Not today,' I grinned, slapping the box of kiddie perm down onto the glass counter.

'Good girl, you're making the right decision,' he answered whilst shoving the box into a plastic bag.

Now I know better, I understand that in that moment, I was making a choice that meant I would be tethered to him or one of his cousin's businesses forever. That's why he was being so nice. I mean, perm is nicknamed creamy crack for a reason. It's the black girl hair gateway drug. It starts so innocently: all you want is a straight, kink-free, 'manageable' mane. But before you know it, it needs retouching because within the next three weeks your roots will come through and reveal the true texture and 'difficulty' of your hair. Don't forget that your regular greases and creams aren't going to cut it, so you need to buy more products.

And finally, just because your hair is now bone-straight doesn't mean it's going to grow ten inches overnight. If you've ever pined after those swinging ponytails on white girls walking down the street or longed for that plump plop of a full head of locks in a hair advert, then you're going to need a little help. And that's where weave comes in. Now we're starting to talk big boy money. This shop owner knew that by trying to conform to Eurocentric beauty ideals, something at the very opposite of the scale upon which I balanced, I would need some assistance – and only his business would be able to sell me what I would need.

But in that moment, I didn't know this. I skipped out of that hair shop just like I had skipped out of the one on Flatbush Avenue many moons ago, but this time it wasn't with innocent, brightly-coloured hair accessories most girls wanted; it was now with the one thing I was sure would make me a loveable black woman.

Hours later, I had to fight back tears.

'Ahhhh . . . my head is on fire!'

'Candice, I told you last night not to go scratching your head. You've aggravated your scalp, so of course it's going to burn,' my mum chastised me as she continued to layer on the thick white cream.

People had told me it would tingle, but this was unbearable. Also, the smell! It was like standing in the middle of a fish market as the floors were being doused in bleach. If I wasn't so concerned with the idea of my head combusting into flames, I would have had to go and throw up for sure.

'Just a little while longer,' my mother pleaded. 'If we wash it out too soon, it won't take and this will all have been for nothing.'

I tried to focus on anything but the burn. I thought about how good I would look. The various styles I would try. How pleasantly surprised my school friends would be. Until, finally, it was time to wash this shit out. The water cooled my head right down.

'That's better,' I said, as my mother went to work at making sure all of the relaxer was washed out.

Mid-wash, I let my hand reach up and touch my hair. It felt . . . light. And, most importantly, kink-free. When it was all over and I looked in the mirror, I couldn't help but smile. It didn't have any product left in it, and yet it laid flat. Honestly, I'd never known why she was spoken about every Black History Month, but looking at my grown-up reflection, I had to admit that Madam C. J. Walker, who had invented the products for straightening Afro hair, was a real G.

But like all new things after a while, the shine began to wear off. Yes, it was easier to just wake up and slick my

27

hair into a bun with some gel and it was nice to feel more mature, but taking care of relaxed hair was hard work. There was the constant retouching, trimming and necessary treatments. The former could be done at home, but the latter really needed professional help.

By then a new salon had popped up less than a ten-minute bus ride away. It had risen quickly in popularity because their prices were very cheap – in most cases they charged less than half of what their competitors did. For schoolgirls like me, it was perfect. Of course, everything that glitters isn't gold, and one of the downsides to the place was that you couldn't make an appointment. When the salon first opened, their business ran on a first come, first served basis. If you weren't there as the doors opened, you could bet that you would be spending your entire Saturday waiting your turn. They then introduced a ticketing system, but it was still a wait. The other downside was that in order to retain as much business as possible, the hairdressers would start on multiple women at the same time, knowing good and well no one was going to leave the shop with their hair only halfway done. It was on one of these particularly busy days that I decided I had had enough.

I was running a little late to make it for opening time, so when I got there the small space was already heaving with girls and women who were intent on leaving looking better than when they arrived. I grabbed a number and waited my turn. Forty-five minutes later, a woman whose name I will never know was slapping relaxer into my head. By now I knew not to scratch my scalp for at least forty-eight hours before getting my hair done, so I was taken aback when the left side of my head started burning. Within minutes, I was yelling so bad that they were forced to stop another woman mid hair wash to make space for me at the sink.

'I keep telling you young girls to not scratch the night before!'

'I didn't scratch my head!' I shouted, bringing all the noise in the hairdresser's to a grinding halt, as everyone stopped talking to listen to me.

I was furious that she was now trying to put this on me. I had been getting my hair retouched for almost a year, I was no longer new to this.

'Matter of fact, let me see the container,' I demanded.

I heard a few mumbles.

'Get me the container!' I yelled again.

Usually, I was reserved and quiet, and that served me well because it meant the girls at my secondary school didn't pick on me so much. But there was something about being surrounded by South London girls with a shit-ton of sass that would come in handy when the time was right. Now was the time. I was livid and embarrassed. I had been a loyal customer to this hairdresser since day one and all of a sudden I was being made to feel like I was in the wrong. Something wasn't right, and sure enough, when a girl who seemed about the same age as me produced the almost industrial-sized container of relaxer, it became clear what had gone wrong.

'Super?!' I cried. 'Super strength?! I always, always use regular.' It was at this precise moment I decided to touch the area on my head that was aggravating me the most. I could feel that the place lacked hair and felt tender to the touch. The relaxer had burned me good and proper. Before my tongue could touch the roof of my mouth, a dark-skinned man I recognised to be the owner stood before me offering his sincere apologies.

'Honestly, we are so very sorry. Please take this treatment on us. We won't charge you this time.'

'This time?!' I snorted, lifting my head out of the sink. 'Trust me, bruddah, there won't be a next time – and while we are here, please let one of these ladies know that I won't be waiting much longer, so someone needs to be about my drying and styling quick.' I kissed my teeth.

Clearly everything I had picked up from my classmates was working because by the time I was making my way from the sink, there was a chair with a different hairstylist smiling apprehensively at me.

'Come, sit down, baby, mek we fix dis.' From her soft tone and intonation, I could tell she was from yard.

When I looked in the mirror, I could see the true damage: a good chunk of hair was missing from my temple and I could see red, raw skin pulsating underneath. I couldn't believe it. The hairstylist must have been surveying my expression.

'Nah worry bout dat, mi see worse. Mi hav one style mek mi gi yuh.' She smiled.

I tried to make myself relax. I had no other choice. For the next half hour or so, I let the lady work her magic.

The moment I stepped out of the shop and into the cool breeze of the afternoon, I promised myself that this would be the end. It was time to break this creamy crack habit before I was left with no hair at all. And although I have to admit I found it hard, I didn't go back on my word.

Over the next few years I tried everything. There were the box braids and Congolese twists, but those hurt like hell and after prolonged styling I started to notice that my hair was thinning around my hairline. There were the trials and tribulations of sew-in weave. I legit only lasted two weeks after I tried to wash and blow-dry it, and the weave ended up getting caught in the fan of my hand-held hairdryer. I had to cut myself free. I decided then and there that I would no longer be fucking around with that either.

There was also a period of just wearing my natural 4C

Afro as it was. It was all well and good during the summer months, but as soon as that harsh British winter swept in, my hair went as dry as the throat of a granny in church who had forgotten her Werther's Originals.

By the time I went to New York for my seventeenth birthday, I had taken to alternating hairstyles between box braids and what my friends affectionately called the 'Alicia Keys' look. This would involve some intricately patterned canerows, and then on the ends I would attach some Afro-style extensions to give them a Powerpuff Girl type look. It was nicknamed the 'Alicia Keys' because in the video for her smash hit song 'You Don't Know My Name', this was the hairstyle she wore as she poured her heart out about a man she wanted to be noticed by.

By now, I had taken to spending a large chunk of the money I was making from being a part-time receptionist on American import magazines which saw African-American women as their target market. I read *Essence* and *Ebony* with a thirst solely reserved for a black girl who was struggling to see herself represented in magazines in her own country. One of my favourite things to do was to look for natural hairstyles I could emulate. I would tear those pages out with such ferociousness, and such regularity, that by the time I arrived in New York, I had over fifty images of hairstyles that I wanted a hairstylist to reproduce for me.

Although it was March, the cold snap that fell over the city was so sharp it burned my throat to stand outside for too long. I had packed one flimsy jacket that wasn't doing very well at keeping me warm. A cousin lent me an ill-fitting coat, and after a few days, she suggested that we ride the train to Queens where she would show me all of the shops selling great brand-name winter wear at a discount price. Stomping from shop to shop in the cold, I couldn't help feeling warm inside as I marvelled at the black culture that seemed to ooze out of every crevice of that place. You couldn't take three steps without a brotha trying to sell you his mixtape: 'You better listen, Ma, Imma be the next Camron, I promise!' or catch young black girls with their hair wrapped to protect it from the harsh elements. There was something about watching their gold nameplate jewellery glisten as they made the same kind of hand gestures I had seen in many hip-hop music videos that just had me transfixed. I hadn't felt it in a long time, but even in that moment when I was cold and unsure of myself, I felt so damn proud to be black.

And then there was a moment I'll never forget. We were about to cross a road, and I was looking at the people around me instead of the traffic.

'Come on, girl, we got the light, keep up before it turns red on us,' my cousin said.

Before I had time to answer, that's when I saw her. Seventeen years later I still remember how much she stood out, as if the whole of Queens had stopped just for her. Medium in both height and build, what hit me straight away was this woman's confidence. It was like a force field. Her black padded coat stopped at the perfect place to give way to her knee-high Timberland boots. But it wasn't her standard NYC winter look that made my jaw drop, it was the way she wore her hair. It was closely cropped and, similar to that of the black men who tried to talk to us every five seconds, faded and shaped up. I had never seen a young woman rock a shaved head before. Sure, it seemed to be the thing to do once you hit a certain age – many black women in their late fifties and early sixties seem to have a penchant for a cropped cut – but younger black women were still not trying to do all of that and being conned into the falsehood that their hair, especially if it was long, kink-free, coolie or 'good', was the essence to their beauty. It would be a reach for me to say all, but I think most of the time and money black women poured into hair styling, hair products and haircare was usually rooted in the idea that a black woman's hair as it naturally grew from the scalp was not good enough. It was as if the kinks and coils of the very strands themselves had to be reshaped so that they fit the standards of beauty Western society knew we could never naturally meet.

There have been recent examples of how these problematic ideas and beliefs still affect people in the UK school system, with many black children of both sexes being excluded because their natural hair somehow goes against school policy. In 2018, Chikayzea Flanders, who was then a pupil at a South London boys' school, was told he had to 'cut off his dreadlocks or face suspension'. A girl called Ruby Williams came out of a long legal battle with her school in East London after repeatedly being told her natural Afro hair was deemed to be against school rules. And it doesn't end there. I have known plenty of black women who have spent more on a new wig than on a new outfit for a job interview as they are very aware how waltzing in with their Afro could be the one thing that costs them the job, even though they are perfectly qualified for it.

Not only does that mean these black women are having to cough up for hairstyles they can't yet afford to try and secure jobs they need by pretending to be something they are not and more than likely don't even want to be, the crippling financial cost is nothing compared to what that does to one's self-confidence. With many black girls from a young age already being conditioned to believe that the only version of beautiful hair is anything but what they naturally possess, it is no wonder that we are all so quick to fall prey to the multitudes of ways we can perhaps 'fix' our hair in the hope of achieving a better quality of life overall.

So, upon seeing this woman in the street in Queens, it was like in one swift move, I was watching someone stick two fingers up to everything: the patriarchy, sexism, beauty standards and expectations. And she looked sublime. Whatever she was doing, I wanted some of that.

'*Candice!*' my cousin screamed, pulling me out of the way of a taxi that had no intention of slowing down for me. 'Girl! You tryna get us killed?! Shit, pay attention!'

'Did you not just see that?' I said, in breathless wonder.

'See what, the taxi trying to squash you?' She laughed.

'No, that woman, that woman with the shaved head. She looked sooooooo good,' I sighed, pulling on the word to make sure she understood the impact of what I'd just witnessed.

'Oh girl, yeah. A couple girls be shaving their heads. But I'm not sure dudes will like that. Don't no man want a woman with less hair than him. So, I don't pay it no mind. It's another fad.' She shrugged.

She stopped in front of a clothes shop.

'Right, let's try this store. You must be freezing . . .' And she marched on through the double doors.

But I was no longer listening. I had finally seen a woman that was an example of the kind of person I was trying to be. I was plotting my next move. I knew it was bold and I also knew few would support me, but it was going to happen anyhow.

The following week, when we arrived back in London, I was desperate to get to a barbershop. I pretended to my mother that I was just popping out to buy something, but my jet lag was still so acute that in my haste, I promptly fell down the stairs.

'Owww,' I moaned, staggering back to my feet.

'Candice, what are you in such a hurry for? You need to chill, we just got back home,' my mother said.

But I was having none of it. Since seeing that queen in Queens, something in me was set alight and the fire had not stopped building and building inside me. Today was the day. And nothing was going to stop me.

I picked myself up and made it to the front door.

'I'll be back soon I just need to pop to the hair shop,' I shouted as I left the house, trying not to think about the fact that I could be coming back only to find I wouldn't be allowed in or, worse still, I'd be getting a big ol' ass-whooping.

Luckily for me, we lived on Somerleyton Estate at the time, which sat bang in the heart of Brixton. And one thing Brixton had many of was barbershops. There were a few I knew because I would regularly take my younger brother to get his hair cut. It was always an uncomfortable experience for me because the men who hung out in these barbershops seemed to be unable to keep their sexual desires in their head. No matter the season, they would wolf-whistle and catcall. I would dress in the most masculine clothes I owned, something baggy, and make myself as small as possible, only making eye contact when it was time to pay. If it was after school and I was wearing my uniform, they took it as a sign to really ramp up their harassment.

'Oh girl, I know you're a baby, but I would love to give you a baby,' one would call out.

'Yes, girl, looking ripe and ready for the picking,' another would echo.

'Don't worry about school, mi will teach yuh,' a third would purr.

Today was different, I was going in for myself, and I was not going to be creeped out by their comments. My first stop was a barber's in the centre of Brixton.

Taking a deep breath, I pushed the door open. No matter the number of times I had been in barbershops, the concoction of scents that assaulted my nostrils always shocked me. It was often a mixture of rubbing alcohol, various eaux de toilette and a lingering hint of weed. The soft punch of the latter was so soft, it was an indicator that obviously whilst no one was smoking it, someone was definitely carrying it.

'Candy girl! What can we do for the little man today?' one of the more regular barbers asked, looking around me and then outside in case my brother was lagging behind.

'He isn't with me,' I said with a half-smile. 'In fact, I was hoping I could get someone to shave my head today.' I spat the sentence out quickly before I had time to chicken out.

A hushed silence descended on the room. If it hadn't been for the soft hum of the television and someone's clippers, I perhaps would have thought Judgement Day had arrived.

'You? Trim fi you?' he asked in disbelief. He then shook his head. 'Nah, nah, yuh mussi mad. I can't do that. Fi yuh muddah fi come kill me? Yuh know how long mi know she? Wha happen? Yuh turn lesbian or dem somethings dere? Yuh need fi fine ah real man. And no bal' head gyal can't keep nuh real man. Man wan fi lie down with feminine woman, not one who favour him.'

And with that he laughed his head off, as did the other men around him.

I felt the tears well up in my eyes, but I was too proud to allow one to fall. Before he could berate me further, I was already back outside the shop. I felt deflated but not deterred. In fact, his passionate tirade about what he would allow to grow out of my head and how it should conform to the style he liked in a woman really pissed me off.

But the next half an hour showed that he wasn't alone in his thinking. I went from barbershop to barbershop, and each one refused to trim me. The excuses varied from me being too young to one even claiming that cutting a woman's hair was against his religion. Each rejection fuelled the fire in my belly even further, and just as I was about to buy clippers and do it myself, I remembered there was one I hadn't tried. It happened to be the one closest to my home. By the time I entered this shop, I had grown confident, but also confident in what their reaction would be. But this one caught me by surprise.

'You sure?' the caramel-skinned barber asked.

'I am sure,' I replied slowly.

'Take a seat then. I tell you what, I'll start at the side, that way if you change your mind, you can turn it into some funky style,' he said, laughing.

'No, thank you. Just start in the middle.'

'Wow, that's fighting talk,' another barber commented.

The barber cutting my hair shook out the black cape like I had seen hundreds of times before, and everything felt so normal and yet so foreign. I had spent hours upon hours in packed, bustling barbershops listening to bro talk. I'd hear the way they rated women as they walked by, I heard passionate arguments about politics and football teams, I'd sat alongside dealers and doctors who all just wanted to get fresh, and now it was my turn.

When the soft buzz of the clippers grew louder, I let out a soft exhale and waited. I waited for my fear of not being pretty enough to drown me, I waited for the expectations of men to scare me out of the chair, I waited for the fear of being judged to propel me to my feet and beg him to stop. But none of those things happened.

Instead in its place came a kind of weightlessness. A sense of freedom. With each stroke of the clipper, I watched my hair tumble to the floor, and not one muscle in my body caused me to bend down and retrieve it. I wanted it gone. As I looked at my face in the mirror, my true black features becoming ever more pronounced now there was nowhere else to look, I felt as though I was seeing myself for the first time since I looked in Veronica's mirror so many years ago. This was who I was supposed to be. Although it would take a while for the world to agree.

By the time I got home, having walked very slowly, every family member in Barbados and New York had heard about how I had 'gone mad', Britney Spears style. I have to admit I don't even think my mother had a problem with it, especially since she was only just beginning to grow locs after years of trying different hairstyles, but I think the fact I hadn't told anyone nor asked for outside opinion was what really annoyed them. And I'll be real, if extended family members who haven't seen you since you were in nappies don't join arms in cussing you when they think you've been disrespectful, then you just ain't where I'm from.

But I stood my ground because I had expected it. I also expected to be taken the piss out of once I returned to sixth form on Monday. So, hearing the entire common room burst out laughing and question whether I was going through chemo or now wanted to 'n'yam pussy' didn't faze me either. What actually threw me was something I hadn't considered at all.

Later that week, it was time to head to my part-time receptionist job. It was at the law firm my father worked at. It could be pretty stressful, especially when there was a big case on. But I had been working there for two years now, so I knew the ropes. Also I had already had my fair share of shitty jobs and even shittier bosses. Whilst I respected the fact that I was a kid who would have to start on the bottom rung of any ladder, it was nice to do a job where no one was looking over my shoulder. The law firm had two offices, one just off of Camden High Street and one closer to Mornington Crescent station. I would begin each shift by going between the two to collect all the post and paperwork that would need filing that day. My dad worked in the Mornington Crescent office and I would always pop in to see him before going about my duties.

His office walls were made of glass. He could see everyone's comings and goings. As I approached the door, I saw his expression change from confused to shocked.

'Hi, Dad!' I smiled. 'What you got for me today?' I eyed up his desk to see if there was any urgent paperwork I would need to take with me.

'Fucking hell, Cand! What have you done to your hair?!' he gasped. 'Good luck trying to find a fella with a look like that.'

My father was never one to mince his words. In fact, he was so cut and dried he often polarised people. You either truly loved his candour or you wanted to slap his teeth down his throat. I clenched my fist to stop me from doing the latter.

'Dad, I'll have you know that I have zero interest in what fellas think of me right now. And even if I did, if he couldn't love me because I perhaps have less hair than him, then I'm probably not missing out on anyone special.'

I promptly left the office without checking again if he had anything he needed me to take. He could walk the shit over himself.

As I strode back to the Camden High Street branch, his questions and distaste rang through my head. How could it be that my father, the one who had always encouraged me to go against the grain and think for myself, had slipped up and showed me that in fact when it came to his ideas and ideals about what and who women should be, he was just as backwards and as sexist as the barbers who didn't want me to cut my hair in the first place? Why did it always seem to boil down to the falsehood that how I presented myself – from the clothes I wore to the hairstyle I chose – had to be for the attention, acceptance and appeasement of the male gaze? Little did I know that choosing this hairstyle was just the beginning of the many ways my choices in life would be questioned.

A few years later, my father apologised. As we both walked the same route from one office location to another, it just began to spill out of him.

'You know, Cand, I have to say sorry,' he began.

I almost tripped over my own feet, as it was so rare to hear these words from him.

'For what?' I asked nervously.

'For being so close-minded when you first did this.' He rubbed my head to help illustrate it was my hair he was talking about. 'To be honest, I was scared for you. It seemed like a big political statement. In my immature opinion, I thought it was a misstep and a cry for attention. I was worried about how other people would view you. But watching you carry yourself like this has been a secret point of pride for me. I know what hair means to black women. And to see you free yourself of that at such a young age has really made me have a good word with myself. You look incredible. Please don't ever change.' He came to a stop and looked me dead in the eye.

'Ah, Dad,' I whispered, trying to fight back the tears.

Little did I know that was the last moment of that kind I would ever have with him. But I carried his words with me everywhere since that day. Hair, especially the hair that grows out of a black woman's head, *is* very political. So much so that when my daughter was born, I was adamant that she never ever felt weighed down, quite literally, by the world's expectations of her and the hair that would also be a part of her. Plus, I had zero hairdressing skills. Because of my short hair, I was so used to just getting up and getting on with my day, without having to worry whether it looked 'presentable' or Eurocentric, that when Esmé was born, I knew without a doubt that I would follow the example many women in my family had set and give her locs. It had taken me so long to understand that not only was my hair acceptable the way it grew out of my head, but it was also beautiful too. I wanted to be sure she felt encouraged and empowered to celebrate her natural hair.

But it wasn't easy. I think there is a falsehood surrounding locs. Many, including myself, believed that it was the easier hairstyle to choose when wanting to sport our natural hair. Nothing could be further from the truth. Upkeeping locs takes work. And between Esmé's unwillingness to sit still during lint-picking sessions, and the demands on my time what with another child and a successful career, we lost our way a bit. Watching her closely during lockdown, I knew the time had come, but I was sure she wouldn't be a willing participant. She was very proud of her hairstyle and it had become not only her signature but also her security. Whenever someone would mention how wonderful her locs were, she would flash them a half-humble smile and say, 'Thank you,' before later telling me how much she loved her hair because others seemed fascinated by it. This worried me slightly. Because now it felt as though the hairstyle – which I had chosen to help free her from the tyranny of a white world's expectations about how a black woman's hair should be – had in another way become a form of bondage, a security blanket. She couldn't bear to think of – let alone see herself – sporting another 'do, and that now worried me more than the judgements and manipulation of the world around her.

I had to be easy with her, build the idea up gradually. I showed her the hairstyles she could finally try that having locs had prevented her from experimenting with. After almost a week of petitioning, she finally relented.

Unbeknown to many, locs don't have to be cut off for the owner to be free of them. There is a more time-consuming but hair-saving way of doing things, and that is by unpicking them. As I said at the very beginning of this lesson, this process would take weeks. Over the course of twenty-seven days, I finally unpicked all the locs in Esmé's hair.

I can't begin to describe the amount of dead hair that came away with each pull of the tail comb. It was remarkable, and also freeing, for the both of us. The change came with a weightlessness that I remembered from when I had my hair trimmed. Usually she would complain of neck ache after having her locs washed. Watching her giggle with glee as her father gave her now-free Afro its first wash, I could tell we had made the right decision. Her hair was no longer boxed in and nor was she. She was now able to experiment with as many natural styles as she wanted whilst continuing to love and appreciate what she had been born with. Would it be the decision she would stand by for the rest of her life? I do hope so, because my scalp had learned the hard way that all those older black women, begging for me not to fall for the creamy crack, or the idea that my natural hair was less than, had been right. But it had been one of the most intricate and revealing journeys of my life. Seventeen years later, I still feel just as refreshed and restored when I get a fresh trim. It's still so very me. But just because I've found myself, I know that doesn't mean I should stop Esmé from going and growing on her own journey. I just hope it's rooted in self-love.

What I wish I'd known:

- Weaves and wigs are not the enemy – the falsehood that we are less than if we choose to wear them is. No matter the hairstyle, you rock, as long as you love and value yourself with or without it, then there really is no problem.

- The male gaze should not be considered when choosing a hairstyle, period.

- Try to not let the opinions of family or friends sway you. I've lost count of the people who once mocked me for wearing my hair closely cropped, only for them to do the same thing a few years down the line. Being a trendsetter can be lonely; do it anyway.

- Where possible, try to buy hair and hair products from black-owned businesses, who not only have greater understanding about your natural hair, but will probably see you as more than just another customer.

- Respect and cultivate a relationship with a hairstylist you trust. 'It's not everyone's hands that should be in your head,' as the saying goes. Finding a hairstylist who really gets you is usually half the battle.

Lesson 2

BATTY & BENCH – ON FRIENDSHIP

'Promise to never take it off?' Jemma insisted, her alabaster cheeks flushing crimson.

'I promise!' I whispered, extending my wrist so she could tie a friendship bracelet around it.

She had spun the purple, blue and green threads into a dense braid before tying the loose ends together to form a circle. As she slipped the bracelet over my wrist, I felt alive – accomplished, even. I had finally found my tribe. It had taken ages.

The tribe in question was the 'Fantastic Five', which was how we were known to our teachers. There was Mo, a tall redhead who wore glasses and had a penchant for finding things preposterous. There was Aisa, a lighter-skinned, heavy-chested black girl who was quite the comic. There was Sarah, quiet and shy, her eyes always peeking out from under a fringe that needed a trim. And then there was Jemma. Jemma was my best friend. She was short like me, which back then was a great thing to bond over. She wore her brown hair in a low-slung ponytail, drank Robinsons squash at playtime and was easily the smartest in the class. No matter the day or weather, you could find all five of us together, usually dissecting the latest storyline in a *Baby-Sitters Club* book. To most of our classmates, we were awkward and geeky, and that suited us just fine.

I still remember the day when I twigged that I wouldn't be able to go to the same secondary school as Jemma. Her parents were well-to-do and her father especially had made it clear that both she and her younger sister were to attend the James Allen's Girls' School after they left primary school. I can't recall how I found out that JAGS was a prestigious private school that cost way more than what my family could ever afford, but I do remember that I was heartbroken.

As the last day of our final term together drew to a close, we wrote each other farewell notes on our school shirts. Having adored watching this ritual from afar for the last six years, I had always assumed that it would feel thrilling and very grown-up when my turn came, but instead I felt nothing but deep sadness. I was afraid to begin again. These were the only friends I had, and we were all going down vastly different paths.

'I promise, you and Jem will see each other over the summer,' Jemma's mother said reassuringly, trying to hold back tears herself.

Jemma and I would not let go of each other's hands. It took a teaching assistant to prise us apart.

'Friends forever!' Jemma called over her shoulder as she made her way to her mother's car.

'Forever!' I yelled in response, as I began to walk home.

That night we spent over an hour on the phone to each other. And true to her word, Jemma's mother ensured the Fantastic Five reunited a few times over the summer. But then secondary school began. I still wore my friendship bracelet. One day, a very cool black girl noticed it.

'Is that . . . a friendship bracelet?' she asked, laughing loudly.

'No!' I hastily responded, pulling my sweatshirt sleeve down quickly. I had been struggling to make friends. I didn't need something as insignificant as some mouldy, tattered piece of wool making it any harder for me.

'OK, if you say so,' she said, giggling, being gracious enough to not press the subject any further.

Walking home that afternoon, I waited until I was alone and then I tugged roughly at the bracelet until the fraying twines conceded to my strength. I looked around me before guiltily throwing it in the bin. That evening, I briefly thought about telling Jemma I had had to take it off, but I didn't want to hurt her feelings.

We tried our best to stay in contact. And for the first few weeks we did well, often speaking to each other at least four evenings a week. But nothing could have prepared us for how time-consuming secondary school was. Those calls soon turned into a once-a-week occasion, and then dwindled to once a month. Until one day, on both ends, the phone just stopped ringing altogether.

The high school I went to was quite the culture shock. Whereas my primary school was very racially diverse, Norwood School For Girls was populated by at least eighty per cent black girls, many of whom felt under pressure to act a certain way to thrive socially. This was new to me. I was used to putting my head down and trying to get high scores on my tests, but here it seemed affiliation and friendships meant way more than working hard. If you wanted a peaceful life, then it would pay to be friends with the cool girls. There was no version of the Fantastic Five here.

Having spent years following strict uniform rules, my eyes grew wide with wonder when witnessing the various ways these girls desperately showed off their personal style. Much of the time, this was through hairstyles. There were backside-grazing box braids (that Rita in *Sister Act 2* look I've mentioned before), a high-piled updo referred to as a 'fan', and canerows which displayed more intricacy than the London Tube map. Just like when I'd been a little girl, ribbons and gems were used as decorative elements. The one thing all of these hairstyles had in common were well-laid baby hairs, with swoops and swirls covering most foreheads.

Jewellery was also used as a status symbol. Although it was against school uniform policy, many of the older girls wore nameplate necklaces and heavy doorknocker earrings. A few Year Eleven students even had gold teeth. For those who couldn't afford jewellery, a cheaper way to show you were rebellious was to wear socks which displayed cartoon characters. Any character would do, but for optimal cool, Kenny from *South Park* was the ultimate winner. To get past the gates, you would have to roll your socks down, well before a teacher who had clearly picked the short straw and was on gate duty saw you, but once you were in, all bets were off and you could bring your A game.

For clarity, I had no A game; in fact, I was borderline Z. I was still geeky and very insular. Whilst many would struggle to believe it given my career now, I am actually very shy. Nothing breaks me out in hives faster than the idea of having to attend a function alone or having to strike up conversation with people I don't know. I am a head-in-my-phone kind of guest. So, no one was more surprised than me when one of the coolest girls in our year took an interest in me.

'Yo, Candice, come here,' she yelled at me during break-time one day.

So many eyes turned to look at me, I felt myself blush. To be at the centre of attention like this was torture for me. Gingerly, I closed my *Harry Potter* book and slowly made my way towards her.

'Yo, why are you always reading?' she enquired, tipping her beautiful face to the side.

I started thinking quickly, aware that my answer might determine my future in terms of social status in this school. Not wanting to dig myself a hole, I shrugged instead.

'Hmm,' she mused. 'I like you. You're kind of shy. You are a bit of a neek [slang for 'geek'], but I think you could be cool.'

The girls sitting around her looked uncomfortable with her decision, but all of them knew better than to challenge her.

'Come, sit with us.' She smiled, a small tooth gem catching the sun and gleaming, just like the one the shorter of the two burglars did in *Home Alone*.

So, that is how it began. The moment that I, the bookish nerd, was initiated into one of the most fiercely protected friendship groups at school was the start of a new kind of education: a lesson that friendships are not always formed out of genuine or similar interests, but sometimes because they are necessary for survival. There was so much these girls did that worried me. They smoked and kissed their teeth at teachers. They were often sent out of class for being disruptive. But they were untouchable. Being friends with them took some of the strain out of what was a complicated and uncomfortable adjustment period for me. So, although it went against every fibre in my being, I took to placing a cigarette behind my ear, wearing socks with characters on and giving teachers a lot of backchat.

Sometimes, when I was standing alone in a hallway because I had been sent out of class yet again, I thought about Jemma, Mo, Aisa and Sarah. It was only Sarah and I who had been sent to less than impressive schools, which regularly came bottom of the school leader boards. I imagined that Aisa had joined her school's choir. I had no doubt that Mo was a member of the chess club and that Jemma had made the hockey team she was so desperate to be a part of. I told myself to push them all to the back of my mind. Those were not my friends any more. And the sooner I stopped thinking about them, the better.

Being welcomed into this new friendship group, this safe space, was the first time I felt that friendship had come at a cost – the price being who I really was. I would pin-point this as the beginning of when I believed that I – the friendship-bracelet-making, *Harry Potter*-reading, perfect-uniform-wearing version of myself – would never be worthy of true friendship, so I thought it best to do away with her forever. Over the next three years, I would move schools once each year. With each one, I added on a newer, firmer layer to my exterior, and an increasing unwillingness to show any softness inside. Whilst true friendship is about trust, understanding and communication, the reality of my life was teaching me the complete opposite.

'You beware of these friends,' an aunt commented one day.

Because my back was turned to her, I was able to roll my eyes without consequence. I had heard this a million times before. It seemed like all this advice had one thing in common: friendships can be bad, and no one is to be trusted. Speaking to a friend whilst writing this, we could not help but meditate on the fact that we were usually offered these tip-offs by people we in turn couldn't trust. I see now that it was yet another remarkable example of gaslighting. We were told that our friends were constant threats to those most would describe as family and that said friends weren't worth the bother at all. I had to remind myself that telling me not to trust anyone, or to see every friendship as a potential time bomb, was also a way to isolate me. But that didn't make me overlook the slither of truth in their general pessimism. I knew for sure that most of the friendships I had been involved in since leaving primary school perhaps weren't the real deal. And I was right.

I remember the day I learned what actual friendship looked like.

By this point, I was a student at BRIT, a well-known performing arts school. During my first few weeks, I had found myself in a friendship group that was a melting pot of misfits. What we all had in common was that we were black, semi-talented in our respective fields, and came from pockets of London that were not privileged in any way. We bonded over our respective shared traumas, which is never a good place to start. Speaking from experience, trauma bonding is never a good foundation upon which to build a friendship.

Some months later, it became clear that one girl in the group, Gabriella, was being bullied by students from her old school. As this was a time before social media, all these messages were passed on to her through others. The increase in unpleasant messages meant that by the time we got word of them wanting to ambush her after school, we were already whipped up into a defensive frenzy.

'Fuck that,' one black girl with locs called Nicole shouted.

Nicole was as short as me and extremely top heavy. Coming from a well-known estate in South London, she gave off the air of being tough and strong, as would befit such an upbringing, and so she had naturally defined herself as the ringleader.

'I say we go there after school and surprise them,' she declared.

We all nodded in agreement. I wondered if anyone had could sense my hesitation. This was way outside of my comfort zone. But I had to play along.

As we made our way down Salter's Hill later that afternoon, we devised a plan. Nicole would go first with Gabriella, and the rest of us would hang back whilst assessing the situation. There were six of us remaining, and we were paired up. My partner was my closest friend at the time, KJ. KJ was tall and broad, with a voice deeper than God's and skin so perfect it was like staring at an oil painting.

KJ had found it hard to fit in. Not just because they were a fan of astoundingly bright clown-like colours, but because KJ had confused people. The baritone of their voice suggested they were male, but they did their make-up better than any female. Although their body type was that of an American football player, they sat with the girls and gossiped about the hottest boys. Even though it was clear they possessed the kind of strength that could spin you out of your trainers, they moved with the innate grace of a prima ballerina. It's clear to me now that KJ was non-binary, but there wasn't the education or understanding back then for what that was. They were comfortable with elements which could define them as either masculine or feminine, but they were not going to be controlled by such definitions.

Upon first meeting KJ, I was in awe. I saw in them what I had long since lost in myself: freedom, individuality, fearlessness. It only took a few weeks for people to call us best friends. I never questioned them, and they never questioned me. That day was to bring us closer together than ever.

KJ grabbed my elbow so that I was forced to slow down. 'You've never done anything like this, have you, babes?' they whispered.

I swallowed and shook my head quickly, not wanting my fear to betray me.

'Listen, this other school know how to rock. Worst comes to worst, you follow me. Do you understand?' they asked, looking down on me with eyes that showed they meant it.

I nodded.

As we got closer to the school, it became clear that the bullies were expecting us.

'Fuck sake, man, who let them know we were coming?' Nicole hissed.

It was too late to wait for an answer. They had spotted all of us. All eight of us. My instinct was to turn and run but the others kept walking forward.

'What are you doing?!' KJ bellowed at Nicole. 'There are hundreds of them, we've already lost, man!' There was an unmistakable tone of fear in their voice. None of us had heard that in their voice before. But Nicole kept marching forwards.

A few students from the school came charging towards us.

'Woah, woah, woah!' Nicole shouted, standing in between Gabriella and the other students. 'Now, we didn't come here for all of this,' she started, her long hair swishing around her head as she spoke.

'Well, it's too late for that, fam,' the tallest of the students retorted, pushing up the sleeves of her blazer.

Before Gabriella or Nicole could say another word, all hell had broken out. Blows began to rain down like hailstones. Soon the main road was overflowing with students who were coming to fight us. Quickly I looked around for my friends, but I could not see them. I closed my eyes and just continued to move my fists. I could feel multiple hands upon me. Some feet too. Someone was tugging on my backpack. I felt myself being pulled towards the floor. The yells and screams were overwhelming. Just as I was about to give up, I felt a well-meaning pull on my arm. I opened my eyes. It was KJ.

'Get up, Candice! Get up!' they ordered.

I saw that they were kicking and punching people as they helped me. Far fewer students had surrounded them. It wasn't surprising at all. Once I was on my feet, KJ covered me like the way Dwayne 'The Rock' Johnson would cover Kevin Hart, which allowed us to fight our way through the thick crowd.

'Right, we have to run now,' KJ instructed, not giving me time to think about it.

I ran as fast as my heavy legs would allow. I was wearing Timberland boots, which was not helpful. A few of the students had decided to chase us. We made a sharp left into a side road.

'Cands! Down here, now!' KJ ordered as they began to slide themselves under a parked caravan. My eyes grew wide with terror. 'Now!' they hissed.

They were right. I knew we had only lost our pursuers for a few seconds.

I quickly threw myself to the ground and inched my way under the caravan, pulling my backpack behind me with moments to spare.

'Where are they?' I heard a boy's voice hiss.

'They deffo came up this way,' a girl responded.

We watched at least five pairs of feet walk quickly past the caravan. We instinctively held our breaths. I turned to look at KJ. For perhaps the first time ever, I saw them. Beneath the grand, bubbly, non-conformist exterior, they were just a normal teenager, who for the first time wore an expression similar to fear. By now we could hear the high-pitched sirens of police cars and the continued yells of 'Fight! Fight! Fight!' far off in the distance.

The clusters of Clarks and Kickers came back.

'Nah, I think we lost them, you know,' someone said.

'Come, we go back and fuck the rest of them up,' the first

boy ordered. And with that we saw the cluster of feet head back in the direction they came from.

We continued to lie still.

'Right, we can't stay here all fucking day,' KJ moaned. 'Come,' they instructed, slowly making their way out from underneath the caravan.

By the time I had rolled out and come to, KJ had already unlocked the side gate to someone's home.

'KJ!' I hissed.

They shushed me with a look that seemed to ask me whether I had a better idea. The truth is I did not. We couldn't possibly head back into that crowd. Not only were we severely outnumbered but we were now also the ones that had gotten away. Only a fool would make a reappearance. I followed KJ into a stranger's back garden.

By now the sirens had grown louder. The surrounding area was definitely hot. Although it was a spring afternoon, I began to shiver.

'Hello! Hello! Hello!' KJ called, using their knuckleduster-covered hands to rap on the glass back door.

'KJ, allow it,' I begged, not wanting to make the situation any worse.

They turned to look at me.

'Listen, C, trust me.'

Just as they were about to knock on the door again, the

face of an old woman appeared. She was a dead ringer for the one in *Titanic*.

'Hello?' she asked, clearly startled by our appearance.

'Uh, yeah, hi. Please can you let us in?' KJ begged.

I almost wanted to laugh. We had already found ourselves on this woman's property without invitation. Now KJ expected this frail white woman to open the door to us? Two black kids who very much looked like they were up to no good? Whilst I had avoided ever getting drawn into all the rumours about KJ, it was now that I could attest that they were from another planet entirely.

The old lady shook her head, pulling back from the glass.

'Please, old lady. My friend and I have been attacked. Can you hear those sirens? That is the police chasing our attackers. Please, just let us in for a few minutes. Please?'

After a few moments of awkwardness, to my absolute surprise, the old lady opened her back door.

'Come in, come in.' She ushered us in, locking the door behind us once we were all huddled in her tiny kitchen.

'Thank you,' KJ sighed with relief.

Perhaps it was delayed adrenaline or the safe respite her kitchen offered, but I began to cry. KJ threw an arm around me.

'C, it's fine. It's fine.'

We both knew it was not. We hadn't heard from the rest of the group. Sirens continued to wail in the background.

As nice as the old lady was being, I knew we wouldn't be able to stay here forever. Even though I had a few scuffles under my belt, I had never been embroiled in anything of this magnitude. What if we were expelled from school? All of these things were racing through my head.

'Oh dear. Well, there is nothing some tea and biscuits can't fix,' the old lady said, flicking on her kettle, clearly not taking no for an answer.

For the next two hours we sat with that old lady as we told her about what had happened and how quickly it had all become so dangerous. In true KJ fashion, they spoke in such a way the old lady ended up telling us her whole life story. Her husband had died, and her children had moved away. But she had lived in the area for decades and was not ready to give up on her independence just yet. By the time we got a text from one of the others, we had eaten all her custard creams.

Later that evening, we all made our way to my home, as I lived within walking distance. Luckily, my mother wasn't home yet. I had never seen my kitchen so full. The eight of us stood there, in stunned silence.

'So, where did you and Candice get to?' Nicole asked, finally breaking the ice.

Without missing a beat, KJ began to enthusiastically tell the group how they had been cornered, but it was I who had jumped in to help them.

'Don't watch C, you know, she's small but mighty.' They all chortled heartily, their laughs echoing around the kitchen.

Soon we were all talking about how hard we had fought, with Gabriella even proudly showing slash marks in her jacket where someone had clearly tried to stab her. Our small crew had been majorly outnumbered. And yet we had all rode out for each other.

'Now that's what you call ride-or-die,' Nicole said, laughing.

I fixed a smile on my face even though I felt so differently inside. I felt we were all united in lying to one another. Because in that moment I couldn't imagine anyone but KJ being bold enough to help me out of a situation that could have potentially cost us both our lives. To then extend their grace further, by ensuring that the friendship group I thought I so desperately needed didn't see me as the weakest link, was true friendship personified.

Even a decade and a half later, KJ and I would retell that story with the same tone filled with protectiveness and passion. Never once did they let on that I clearly wasn't about that life. KJ took that one to their grave. I miss them, but for that lesson in what true friendship looks like, I am forever thankful. Because there were other versions of friendship that I was yet to experience.

When I was in my twenties, my father said something that rattled me.

'Cand, if you have the same friends at thirty as when you were fifteen, something is wrong. One or two at a push is fine, but any more than that, and either yourself or your friends aren't evolving. Being stagnant is no good for anyone.'

I sighed and cut my eyes. What did he know, anyway? Dad had two friends that I knew of, and they both had the same name, so it was kind of like a buy-one-get-one-free deal. Other than that, he had a great way of keeping everyone at arm's length. But I had a vast group of friends. By now the internet was in full swing, which meant finding people who had shared interests was far easier. Current friends introduced me to new ones, so I never felt as though I didn't have a big enough social circle, even though the quality of the friendships was sometimes questionable.

Indeed, apart from KJ, I seemed to have a knack for attracting friends who took far too much pleasure in putting me down. There was the friend who always had something to say about my weight. The friend who made me feel bad for not going to university, not being in an established relationship and not having 'proper' career aspects. There was the friend who routinely mocked my height and then got big mad the day I snapped and called her a jolly black giant. But I didn't see these as red flags. Belittling, competitive friendships were the only ones I knew and all that seemed available to me. I would never be the smartest, thinnest, prettiest or coolest, so in some regard I felt lucky to have any friends at all.

But as time went on, it began to dawn on me that my dad was right. Apart from KJ and one other mate, a lot of my friendships had changed. Those I would have once declared to be my besties no longer called my phone – hell, none of them have even met my children. Being the first one in my friendship group to become a mother definitely made me feel as though I had been cut adrift. All of a sudden, I couldn't partake in drug-fuelled all-nighters or sleep in until midday. Shit, I couldn't even go to a coffee shop without drawing up a floor plan first to ensure I could get the buggy into the place without difficulty.

Watching those I once partied with go on to hang out with those we once spoke ill of made me deeply uncomfort-able. As I once heard, 'I don't care what a stranger has said about me; what I have to question is why that stranger felt comfortable saying ill shit about me to you when you're my friend?' As clipped and chaotic as those friendships were, they helped me to learn how to be a better friend. Now, I try to be honest about my ever-evolving personal attributes and values, and I always consider the following questions when thinking about a friendship:

Do I actually like this person?
Do they make me feel like we're in competition with
    each other?
Do I actively want to spend time with them?

Becoming a mother made me really think about these things, because now the friends I made or stayed connected to weren't just about me – in many ways, they had to act as a support system for my family too. And as I often say – whilst I sometimes struggle to make the best choices for myself, when it comes to being Esmé and RJ's mum, I am that bitch. For a while I struggled with loneliness whilst I worked my way through trying to be the best friend I could be to myself and my kids.

I remember early on in my adult life I initially made the huge mistake of confusing working relationships for personal ones; spending eight hours a day plus in an office can do that to you. I remember the day I finally plucked up the courage to try and make friends with another black woman in one of the many offices I would work at over the years. The rejection was swift and sharp. Her absolute horror at me trying to ask about her Jamaican upbringing was clear for everyone to see. In my head it was perhaps the thing that could have bonded us; we could have broken the ice with our sameness and in that moment our otherness. But instead, her walls went up, which immediately confronted me with another warning I had heard when I was growing up.

'And for the love of God, don't become friends with black people. They don't want to be your friend. They are jealous and black-hearted. Staying away from them will save you some heartache.'

I think by now it should be no surprise to you, dear reader, that the person who offered up that information was of course as black as I am. By then, I was used to this kind of dialogue. It was loud and clear that 'we' couldn't trust our 'own'. Listening to elders tell it, 'we' were always out to hurt or harm one another – especially in workspaces where there weren't enough seats at the table. Black people couldn't be friends with one another because we were always going to be each other's competition. There could only ever be one black boss at any given time.

In fact, all I could see is that there were *no* black bosses. Hierarchically speaking, most of those jobs proved that those who looked like me only seemed to get so far. When the time came to talk about roles that had titles such as director or partner, there wasn't a black face to be seen. So, whilst that black colleague's rebuttal cut deep, I not only understood it, I respected it.

As I moved from working in an office space to working for myself, finding friends who looked like me was even harder. Not because they weren't there, but because working online was even more cutthroat than I had expected.

'Girl, if you wanted to write a tell-all about how many black women in this industry have tried to stab you in the back, you would run out of paper,' a close friend said over drinks, laughing. Of course, she was black, because this wasn't a conversation I was trying to have with anyone who wasn't. It was inside talk, family business, sista to sista kitchen table chit-chat. We both knew that those stories, very much like the one that KJ could have told about me, were going nowhere. Now, of those who have been unkind even though we share sistahood, let me say I understood their actions completely because I too have fallen prey to the idea that when it comes to climbing any type of ladder, two of us is far too much. I have actively had to rewire my brain and make conscious decisions to not immediately see my sista as a threat but as a partner. Of course, this queen bee syndrome happens regardless of race, this idea that there are fewer spaces for women, period. But throw blackness into the mix and now we aren't talking about a space, we're talking about a crevice, a slither of an opening that you need to get good at making yourself small enough to fit through. From the looks of things, you couldn't get half your person through, let alone another black woman. So it was better to be safe than sorry.

Of course, there were times when I wanted to take to the internet to shout about how someone I thought was a friend turned out not to be so. But firstly, it happened so often that, a bit like crying wolf, repeatedly sending for people would quickly lose its effect. And secondly, I had to admit my part in all of this: my desire to please and be of service was something that had caused detrimental imbalances in past friendships.

These days, my intuition is helping me navigate the fact that some friendships haven't been that great, but that doesn't mean that I should freeze people out entirely. Perhaps it means I should be slower to develop deep connections that aren't just rooted in shared trauma or the dislike of someone else. Because let me tell you about that last one: if you became someone's friend based on your mutual dislike for someone else, that is not your friend. That is merely a reflection of your low self-esteem in human form. And I do not say that to throw shade; instead, I say that so I can take my place right there in the sun. I too am guilty of forming alliances with others based on the vacuous validation I could receive when verbally tearing someone else down. Take it from me, there are better ways to spend your time. My grandad always used to say that 'a dog who will bring a bone will also carry one' and I think this speaks volumes about those kinds of friendship: if you aren't careful, it could be you next.

And it has happened to me. I have been horrifically trolled online by someone who has been in my home and held my children. I have watched an ex-friend gather with those who at one point in time we agreed were the enemy. What all those past connections have in common is that we both decided to become friends when we were very unsure of ourselves. How else was it going to end?

Recently, a woman asked me about what she should do because a very close friend of hers was not responding well to her success. I went down the empathetic route, as I've been on both sides of that coin. I have been jealous of my friends who seemingly have their lives together and I've been the one that friends are jealous of. What is true, though, is that any friendship that ignites jealousy is forever changed. Now, if you are able to work through those changes, that is fine. But most cannot withstand such feelings. The process of struggling to find friends when I moved from the playground to the boardroom has continuously shown me that the best friendships develop when both never want what the other friend has.

It's the Oprah and Gayle version of friendship. The type where you will both privately correct each other but always publicly support each other. It's the type where you will be respectful of each other's differences whilst also leaving enough space to learn from each other. And most importantly, it is the type of friendship that can go the distance because neither desires what the other one has. Separately, they are enough. Together, they are dynamite. I had always admired those kinds of friendships from afar. Especially those between black women. They seemed like unicorns. But it had quickly become clear that looking for a sista in the adult world was not going to be easy either.

Like most things, my Gayle appeared when I was not paying attention.

Honestly, she's one of the reasons you're holding this book. She's a true cheerleader and champion, but it took time for me to see this. The warnings and past experiences deep in the back of my mind almost stopped the friendship from flourishing, but time after time Gayle really showed herself to be a real . . . G. I have lost count of the times someone has tried to be mean or backstab me in her presence. She shuts it down immediately. And even though I haven't had to endure as much obvious negativity being directed her way, I've found myself standing firm for Gayle as if she were family. Which is why we have both made a verbal and written pact to stand in as guardians for each other's children should the worst happen. It is why we are both down as each other's emergency contact for various things. It is why I have no doubt we will go halves on a holiday home later down the line. Sometimes, you just know.

My friendship with Gayle restored my faith in developing relationships with others out of choice and love. Alongside Gayle, I have four other people with whom these kinds of offerings are commonplace. But they do not come easy. A lot like romantic relationships, friendships take work. They need pillars like support, reciprocity and openness. And most importantly, they need constant communication. It always shocks me to hear how many rules, expectations and boundaries people have for their future significant other but when it comes to friendships, they fall mute. Whilst most of my friendships disbanded because they were very obviously seasonal, there are a few – perhaps two – which could have been saved if we had incorporated some of these pillars.

And then there are the friendships that would have perhaps lasted longer if I had been better at communicating. There have been friendships which have died a slow death because of my dislike for responding to texts or answering the phone, my inability to get back to people.

As I watch the phone ring, I promise myself that I will call back tomorrow, which I never do. Days roll into weeks, weeks morph into months and before I know it, I've neglected a friendship to the point of no return. I take no pride in this. My reluctance to reciprocate when it comes to communication means that I have less to bring to the friendship table. The few friends I do have are well versed in my antics.

'Sis, I was about to drive to your house and let off a flare,' a friend joked recently. I had seen her texts for the last couple of days and made a mental note to return her call. But Bode had gotten there before me. She had decided to call him, just to check if I was OK.

'I've known you since reception, so believe me when I say

that I'm used to your nonsense, but girl, you ain't even on socials right now. You have to let people know you're good,' she sighed.

We spoke for forty minutes and it was heavenly. I had to end the call abruptly because RJ was pushing his fingers in plug sockets.

'Girl, I'll call you later!' I assured her.

'No, bitch, you won't, but that's fine, I still love you.' The line went dead with us both knowing she was right.

But she was one of the rare people who understood that communication was not a deal-breaker in our friendship.

Speaking of communication, there is also something to be said for online friendships. Having matured during a digital age, forming friendships online has never been something I have been snobby about. As I grew up, there seemed to be very little advice when it came to making friends outside of playgrounds and schoolyards. And when you feel as though you can really be yourself online, it seems to be an easy way to form connections that can lead to true friendship. For someone like myself, making a friend in a digital space has sometimes felt far more comfortable than trying to maintain a connection IRL.

But can you really be mates with someone you've never met? I mean, we've all seen *Catfish*, right?

Yeah, outside of those who feel so unconfident about who they are they have to patrol the online streets in disguise, I think fabulous friendships can grow – I know this, because it's happened for me. This person is not only there for me, but also for my children. She has a heart of gold and is one of the first people I turn to when I'm feeling a bit blah. And no, we have never met. We may never meet. But I put her right up there with the KJs of my world. A true rider. Being friends with her has also made me think about life outside of my able-bodied privilege. Through her, I have learned that for some, online friendship is the only version they may ever know. And who am I, who are we, to say that lack of physical touch invalidates someone's love? Being friends with her has really made me respect how sacred online friendships can be. I know how precious it is.

As we'll see in Lesson 4, I know a thing or two about online friendships, and how they can be less than stellar experiences. Much like the pre-teen I was decades ago, I have often made the mistake of thinking that everyone in the digital world is a friend. Lavishing them with kindness and respect, immediately thinking they too would return the favour.

'It really is the expectation that gets you hurt, babe,' Bode sighed, offering me a tissue to help mop up my sobs.

Moments before I had found out that yet another online 'friend' had betrayed me.

'I . . . just . . . don't . . . get . . . it,' I cried. I felt sad and very silly.

'I don't know how many times I have to tell you that these aren't your buddies. They are your colleagues. And some – no, many – believe you to be their competition. The quickest way to feel better is to remember that no one owes you anything. You really have to hold back more.'

He was right. For so long I had used several things – men, money and clearly friendships – to help prop up my self-worth. I had to understand that it was not the quantity of those I had around me but the quality. Being a beg friend was not cute. As the elders would warn, 'Every skin teet, weren't a laugh', which means not to trust someone just because they appear to be friendly. And as much as that went against my innate desire to be liked and accepted, it was time to pull back on the online schmoozing before it was too late. These online cronies didn't have to be loyal to someone they didn't know.

So now I keep the majority of online interactions to exactly that. We are simply ships passing in the World Wide Web waters. In time, a gentle current will pull us in different directions. I have learned the hard way how to be cool with that. Although it can feel awkward being on a set with a group of people who appear to be really close, I know the truth. And that momentary twinge of loneliness is quickly cured when I acknowledge that I do not have to worry about someone befriending me only to stab me in the back a few months down the line.

Over the last few years, I've really cultivated a wonderful group of friends, only two of whom have known me for years. I guess Dad was right: if life is chugging along and you are changing and being challenged, it's only right that this group of people will change. And that's no bad thing. It's no bad thing at all.

What I wish I'd known:

- A framework of what you desire should not solely be reserved for romantic relationships. Have expectations and set boundaries, in friendships also.
- A bit like expensive beauty products, a little goes a long way. When it comes to friendships, it's not about how many you have, it's about how solid they are.
- Not everyone is a bredrin. Some are comrades or colleagues.
- As saccharine as it sounds, work on being your own best friend first and foremost.

Lesson 3

BLOODLINES – ON FAMILY

Blood isn't always thicker than water. The end.

Lesson 4

**TWEET, LIKE, SHARE, DELETE
AND REPEAT – ON SOCIAL MEDIA**

As I begin to write this, I am three days into my nine days of annual leave. Aside from recently well-documented family holidays, this is the first proper break I've had since 2017. And the biggest reason why this moment of respite feels so unique is because for the first time in almost four years, I'm not beholden to any algorithm. I am completely unplugged. I'm not taking time off whilst trying to perfect my poolside selfie. I'm not using these down days to bulk-shoot content. And I'm not worried about what anyone will think of my absence. I've spent the last three days sleeping, eating cheese and having way more sex than usual, and it has been heavenly. Because I've taken a break from social media.

The thought of doing this even a few years ago would have perhaps brought me to tears. I am part of the MSN-chat-room generation. You know, the times when having the internet connected to your 'big back' home computer was still a luxury. I still remember my mother's salty tone once she finally got through to me on the phone as she made her way home to instruct me to get the chicken out of the freezer or something. She'd had to call incessantly, because Wi-Fi was still a distant dream, and the only way I could download pixellated images of the friends I had just seen at school was to unplug the house phone, plug in the modem and prepare to surf the net.

When money got particularly tight and there was no internet at home, I would amass some change from my lunch money and spend all my spare time in an internet cafe. Things changed quickly. My first taste of social media came via a website called hi5, but really it was still just a speck in Silicon Valley's eye. After that there was Face-pic and then came the juggernaut that was MySpace, made by a dude simply called Tom. It was a phenomenon. All of a sudden, my friends and I felt compelled to be 'logged on' constantly. That flashing little green person-shaped icon let all your friends know that you were now online, and the instant rush that swept over me when I noticed someone I liked was online too was intoxicating.

Whilst the entire thing was quite arbitrary and the social exchanges so vacuous they were forgotten overnight, one thing that I learned quite quickly was how useful this new platform was at helping me promote my work. By work, I speak of short stories and poems I was writing, which I was sure were going to make me a bestselling author in a heartbeat. Blog posts were all the rage for showing a user's flair for words, and I was hooked. I wasn't alone in quickly learning how powerful this promotional platform was. With musicians such as Lily Allen, the Arctic Monkeys and Kate Nash ('Foundations' is still such a banger) all using MySpace to help them grow a fan base, which offline would have taken a street team of thousands, we, the LimeWire generation, were heading for the place of no return, and we didn't even know it.

Of course, soon MySpace was overtaken in popularity by something created by a guy who looked like he could have been best friends with Tom at the time, and that something was Facebook. But hot on its heels was another platform called Twitter, which coincided with us now having phones which kept us connected twenty-four-seven. I saw the distinction between Facebook and Twitter to be very clear. Facebook was the family reunion and Twitter was the prom's after-party. I would use the former to keep people updated about what I was doing, and the latter to talk about what I wanted to do. It didn't occur to me that on both these platforms, my deepest teenage thoughts – which were once only really shared between best friends and those super shit diaries with the useless locks that never deterred my mother from taking a peek – were now floating about in the ether for all to see. It didn't matter. It was Zuckerberg and Dorsey's world; we were all just visiting, dipping in and out whenever we were at work, school or at a friend's home who had steady internet.

I remember when my relationship with the internet and these social media sites changed forever. Those of you who read *I Am Not Your Baby Mother* will be familiar with some of this story, but not everything. I thought I'd go into more details here.

Sitting at the imposing computer screen of my then host family in Naples in Italy, I did the rounds. I had the day off, as they all – including the two children I was an au pair for – had gone to Rome for the day. As usual, they had invited me but I had decided to sit this one out. I had been in Italy almost three months and I was struggling. There was a distinct level of anti-blackness that permeated the air wherever I went. And the fact that I was still struggling with basic Italian really made me an outlier. I was safe in the apartment, plus I had some emails to send and my Facebook and Twitter accounts to check. The weather was lovely, but I had long since been chased off the balcony by the angriest crow. So, with my third espresso keeping me company, I hopped between my email inbox, Facebook and Twitter, to keep up with and connect with friends and family.

A little while later, I noticed some private messages on Facebook which made little sense to me. The bulk of them were from my dad's colleagues. Each one was asking me to contact them urgently. I had emails from them in my inbox too. With the penny still lingering in mid-air, I quickly sent my father an email asking him to have someone at his office check their server, as it seemed as though they had been hacked. And then I went back to mindlessly scrolling through the Twitter timeline, before heading back to my Facebook page to upload some pictures I had taken on my digital camera the night before.

The next half an hour saw my life shift so dramatically that it's only almost a decade on that I can evaluate all the layers that made up this pivotal moment. My father had died. And having no other way to contact me, his colleagues had taken to my social media to urge me to make contact. In the midst of my crushing new reality, all the pieces had found their place when I was finally told the truth in black and white:

'Candice. We are trying to reach you desperately because – and Jesus, I wish it didn't have to be like this – but your dad has died. Please, please call me urgently on . . .'

Of all the digital communications that have ever reached me, that was by far the most sobering. And now looking back, that is when I learned how powerful this new thing was. There I was, trying to live my best twenty-year-old life in a new country, grappling with an intricate language and unfamiliar surroundings, and when something life-altering happened in my home country, people had gathered in this new space to get my attention. Perhaps because my host family were a four-hour drive away and I couldn't get hold of any of my Italian friends, I found myself instantly reporting every emotion I felt to the internet. The instantaneous out-pouring of support was remarkable. Whilst I would have given anything to have real people in the apartment with me, this consolation prize was keeping me afloat.

Through tears, I read sweet messages from old school-mates like Jemma and Aisa, who had never even seen my adult teeth come through. Strangers were leaving comments telling me how they too had just lost a parent and they were praying for me. My father's friends and colleagues told me how proud he had been of me. And all of this was happening in real time. In that moment, I truly felt the magic of what social media could provide, and have never forgotten the sheer love and support that enveloped me then and there. Even if the sheer public vulnerability of it all would more than likely have sent my father running for the hills had he been alive to see it. Years after he died, I dedicated many fruitless hours to trying to find his digital footprint, of which there wasn't even an outline of a toe to be found. He hated being in front of the camera, although he loved to be behind it, making me his subject. My innate flair for being on-screen, combined with his love of making home movies on his beloved JVC handheld camcorder, perhaps explains a lot about my career now. He would have been amazed and appalled that even now, long after his flesh has turned to dust, his end – and by default, his beginning – lives on because I decided to share everything online the instant I'd read about his death.

Fast-forward to a new app on the scene by the name of Instagram. With iPhones quickly replacing the cantankerous Blackberry as the must-have mobile device, I was only too happy to say goodbye to the fragile tracker ball and also my digital camera. Now phones came with a camera, and Instagram was one step ahead when it came to forecasting just how much of our lives we would want to share in a visual sense. With the new ability to take pictures to support my tweets, keep my Facebook page updated and 'create content' to add to the hottest new social media platform, the need to seem and stay connected was at fever pitch. All of a sudden everything felt so considered. My friends and I couldn't just go out to eat, we had to think about whether the dishes looked Instagram-worthy, whether the lighting was good. We had to carefully consider the clothes we would wear . . . With every inch of our lives potentially shareable, planning was key.

And with almost lightning speed, Instagram became a place where you could not only put your life out there, but you could also make money from doing so. I noticed very early on how those who had used blogging as a way to carve out a career for themselves were now doubling their efforts on this app because there was potentially a lot to gain. And I wanted in. I have never held back from showing that – from the very beginning of my content creator journey – I wanted to be able to use this platform for advertising too. There are some who, for whatever reason, would never be so forthcoming with that information. But I was a working-class black woman from South London. In some ways that was my privilege. I didn't have to pretend that I had it made or that I simply got lucky; I could say with my chest out that I was here to better the life of my family, and there was something remarkably freeing about that.

If you only post pictures of your cat or use social media to catch up with or spy on old schoolmates, then the next few thoughts may mean very little to you. But I doubt that. The mention of social media and those who create the content we all inhale (now more commonly known as influencers) always provokes an array of different opinions and emotions, but also curiosity. I have found that even friends who only use it for said pets and the stalking of exes can't help but want to know more about what goes into the building and maintaining of an online audience. With that said, if you have been skim-reading this bit to get to when I reveal the magical six steps I took to build my own personal brand – a kind of *Idiot's Guide to Making It on Instagram* – then I will put you out of your misery right now.

Sis, there is no such thing.

No such thing.

Off the top, if there is one piece of advice I can give you, it's *do not* spend what little money you may have to pay someone who claims they can provide you with a magic formula. It's all poppycock. There is no 'grow an audience quick' scheme. Another falsehood is that you will stumble into an online audience just by following your passion and getting lucky. That's bullshit too. Take it from someone who knows. It's actually quite the opposite. It takes planning, commitment and a layer of skin thickness that would befit an alien. Yes, a sprinkling of luck for good measure can be helpful. But success in this realm is nearly always down to hard work. There will be reasons why someone's platform may grow quicker than another's and you can obviously attract more eyeballs to your page with a few clever strategies. But none of this replaces the blood, sweat and tears (of which there are a lot) that go into creating engaging content in the first place.

In fact, the first thing I ask people who want to know how they can grow their social media audience is: 'What do you want out of this?' You know that scene in *The Notebook* where Ryan Gosling is yelling, 'What do you want?!' That is me right now, asking you this. It scares me how many current content creators or those who believe they want to be 'influencers' have never thought about this.

Before I decided to quit a job in marketing in a publishing house and devote most of my life to essentially marketing myself full-time, I had a very clear plan laid out. One I have always been honest about, too: I'm in, out, shake it all about, do the hokey-cokey, make some millions and gracefully get the fuck out. Because even if this way of doing business lasts forever, my patience to withstand the negativity which comes with it will not. But more on that a little later on.

Having spent years around award-winning marketers, I picked up on a gap in the market pretty early on. One of my tasks was to go through a list of a hundred or so bloggers and enquire as to how much they would charge to advertise a new title the publishing house was releasing. Typing their websites and Instagram handles into search engines, I think it was by about the twenty-fifth image of a white woman that I started to realise that none of these bloggers were anything other than white. I carried on, praying for anything that offered up some variety.

By the time I had reached the end of that list it became clear that the blogging space wasn't diverse at all. I couldn't help but wonder if I possibly had what it took to do what they were doing and by the sounds of the responses to my enquiries, they were getting paid very well to do so, too. Advertising by way of social media was not only cheaper for brands than taking out double-page spreads in magazines and renting billboards, it was also way more trackable, in that businesses would be able to get concrete answers in regards to how many viewers had seen their adverts. Add to the equation the fact that they could tap into a ready-made audience who trusted in the opinion of a person they followed, and it's an advertising match made in heaven, a business model that's showed no signs of slowing down. Influencer marketing growth is up year-on-year and we have seen plenty of content creators go on to build multimillion-pound and -dollar businesses.

Even with the Covid-19 pandemic, interest and investment in influencer marketing has gone undisturbed. If anything, it seems to be quite the opposite. All of a sudden, with lockdowns, furlough and tier systems, everyone's eyes were glued to their phones. Businesses quickly pivoted to online campaigns rather than outdoor ones, because even if you passed their poster whilst out for your one hour of allotted exercise, more than likely you weren't going to pay it any interest. If you were lucky enough to have built a solid online audience already, your gig was safe.

What most either fail to recognise or choose to ignore is that building a community of any kind takes work. Even the most flippant content takes time to go viral. And – now this is the mindfuck – just because you've gone 'viral' doesn't necessarily mean you can quit your day job. That part – the part that keeps people coming back to your social spaces – that part takes tremendous work. Establishing a rapport with your audience takes years and trying to sell them anything will take even longer.

Developing a career using the internet is not for the faint-hearted for a myriad of reasons.

Firstly, this isn't like the old days when people wrote fan mail through the post. As you'll all know, it's all much faster and spontaneous, and the same quickness with which someone can adorn you with appreciation and well wishes is the same as when another tells you to go and kill yourself. Never before have we lived through a period where so many people have shared their views at any given time, and not only can this be difficult for obvious reasons, it's also important to analyse what this does to the person at the receiving end.

I know this all too well because for many years, as I tried to grow my online audience and establish clarity with regards to my personal brand, I often found myself moving far away from what I initially set out to do, because it seemed that I wasn't able to please everyone. And as a firstborn with raging attachment issues, this was devastating. A negative comment would pop up just as I was thinking about a new idea or celebrating a personal achievement, and promptly ruin my day. I became obsessed with trying to come across as being something for everyone.

But then I realised that I wasn't a stocking filler, I was a living and breathing human whose opinions and mind changed as regularly as my knickers did, so this meant that this approach was futile. The only way I was going to succeed at not only retaining an audience, but also crossing over into mainstream media, was to be my damn self. No gimmicks, tricks or gloss. Just me. For anyone who has read up to here and still thinks they want to use social media to build their career, my most important tip therefore is that being yourself does pay off. It gives you the freedom to create the content that will resonate, and also provides the roots you will need to stand firm in the face of adversity or scandal, which there will inevitably arrive no matter how 'unproblematic', 'un-opinionated' or 'neutral' you view your brand to be.

Indeed, trying to use the internet to pay your bills comes with a whole new level of fuckery when you're a black woman. In the tangible world, as black women, we know our margin for error is slim, and that's when we are working in an office with a HR department. But online, that margin is non-existent. Sexism, racism and a nice salt-bae sprinkling of misogynoir are really apparent when you dare to show up online as a black woman. I have lost count of the many ways in which I am racially abused. And I am not alone in this; Labour MP Diane Abbott is a perfect example for how much harsher the internet can be towards black women. Past research by Amnesty International* found that Abbott received 45.1% – almost half – of all the abusive tweets sent to female MPs ahead of the 2017 general election. These weren't just limited to racial abuse; Diane Abbott also regularly received rape and death threats.

I learned a long while ago that Twitter is an alarmingly unsafe place for those who aren't white, cis and heteronormative. Having found myself on the receiving end of some hurtful tweets around the time of the publication of my first book, I finally felt it was time to leave a party from which I no longer was able to glean any joy: the Twitter party. Twitter feels like a room with only one door, no windows and a shit-ton of people more intent on airing their views than listening to anyone or anything else.

Although in my opinion, Twitter is the worst of all social media platforms when it comes to trying to avoid unkind interactions, it is not a unicorn. Unfortunately, the immediate

---

* 'Black and Asian women MPs abused more online', Amnesty International UK, 2018

anonymity of the internet means that no matter what corner of this vast web you decide to occupy, there is the potential for you to have a neighbour who just doesn't take a liking to you. It's at this point that I must remind you that you are entitled to abundant use of the block button. Whilst there are other measures in place to keep harmful words at bay, I say go straight to removing harmful people from your online life completely. What would you do if someone came into your home with their shoes on, ignored invitations to leave, proceeded to shout at you whilst you tried to make them a friendly cup of tea and then finally, just for laughs, pulled down their pants and began to defecate on your kitchen floor? Exactly. Next time you wouldn't open the front door, right? So I often wonder why we are so relaxed about our online boundaries.

I think the eye-opening moment was when RJ was a few months old and we decided to get a babysitter. I had idly posted about the fact that I was going to have a night out. I remember reading some unkind words which sent me into a meltdown. Back then I hadn't yet clocked that nothing and I mean *nothing* feeds trolls more than crying on the internet. It is indeed their protein shake of choice. Unable to leave, crying, confused and clutching my baby to my breast, I tried to reason with strangers through my phone screen about why I thought it was important to have some baby-free time. Writing this now, I flush hot with chagrin. So addicted was I to this all-consuming way of sharing and entertaining, thinking that I owed someone, anyone, an explanation. In the heat of the moment I thought that was the right thing to do. If I could reach back to that point of my life, I would pull myself up, switch my phone off, jump in a hot shower, go out and have the time that I not only deserved but was entitled to. And not cared what anyone thought of that. But we only do better once we know better, and it's taken me years to modify my boundaries when it comes to social media.

Speaking of likes, I was once addicted to seeing how many of those I could rack up. This led to a detrimental impact on my mental health too. No matter how well things were going in the real world, if the Instagram algorithm couldn't confirm my greatness, I would be bereft. For weeks, I would devise ways that I could get this invisible system to agree to my brilliance. After another fourteen days of trying to impress the 'like' gods by constantly creating and spending all my spare time on the app, I would finally be rewarded with a huge dump of likes on a post that I had been sure would flop. Now, of course, I am annoyed with the way that a machine chooses to show us what we want to see and we no longer get to decide that for ourselves, but I'm committed to remembering what is within my control and what I consume and how often I do so. And anyway, likes were not the only thing I was obsessed with – I of course was kept awake by thinking about how I could grow my following too. This feeling was permeated by others constantly bringing the matter up.

'Your content is so good, why don't you have more followers?'

'Why is it that this person has millions of followers, and you don't?'

'Oh, that's good, but I was speaking with someone the other day who had five million followers, isn't that awesome!'

To most of these questions, I now just shrug and say I don't know why my following isn't as big as others. But the truth is, I do. Again, a lot has to do with race, but unlike Twitter where it's more straightforward, with Instagram there are subtle complexities that I feel I need to spell out: I am a dark-skinned black woman, not in an interracial relationship, who doesn't know where to start with a lace front nor cares about getting a smaller waist and bigger ass.

Shit, did she just go there? I hear you gasp.

Yes, sis, I did.

The fact is, I am absent of all the bells and whistles that make for super speedy growth hacks. I don't have children that can be categorised as 'exotic' and so there is no reason to fetishise them. I'm not with a 'spicy' white man we can pretend to invite to the cookout when he posts a black square and can help dissolve me of the obvious blackness that lingers in the air as a threat, I do not possess the artistic ability or expertise to be the next best beauty blogger or hairstylist, and even though I have toyed with the idea of getting a BBL, like most who are naturally blessed with larger posteriors, nothing makes me feel more comfortable than dressing like an Amish milkmaid.

So I'm left with myself: an obviously black woman who likes to talk about raising her very black children, about how we can all be better allies for those who look like me, all finished off with a sprinkle of fashion and beauty the way I like it. That kind of content isn't always relatable or popular. Nor is it always something that can be easily digested or humorous. It is layered, complicated, rich and impactful. And it's that last word that means the most to me.

Impactful.

It's taken me years, but I now fully understand the significance of the expression 'quality over quantity'. I have truly seen that – not just in what I am able to produce and promote, but also in other people's work I admire. Yes, I may not be the most popular person on the block, but I have clear intent because, as previously mentioned, I have learned to be myself, which naturally leads to longevity on and off social media, and that for me is the sweet spot.

Another thing I've learned: when the shit hits the fan, it

is usually centred around whom you've decided to collaborate with. I found myself at the centre of such a storm when I chose to work with a brand which produced formula milk. Surprising to me – perhaps because where I came from, you just got on with feeding your baby whichever way you could – there were many people who deemed this advert as immoral even though I had always been clear about both my children being bottle-fed. Watching my comment section turn into a boxing ring was like nothing I had ever experienced.

'I just don't understand it,' I said to a friend. 'They do know I gave my children formula. How can this ad possibly be so aggravating?'

'Girl, it's because most of those opposed are privileged enough to do so,' she explained.

She was right. It was a certain type of person who was ticked off. And whilst I could get over that, what didn't sit well with me was that some of those who were posting some of the nastier comments to publicly berate me had my personal contact details. I had wrongly assumed they were my friends.

As much as feeling betrayed in that moment hurt, I was able to stand firm because I had not upset my own moral compass. And that's why, if you search hard enough, you can still find the ad today. But there remains a lesson to be learned: you could be as ethical, unproblematic and careful as possible, but people don't need that big of a reason to be pissed off, and you have to take the rough with the smooth. That was one of the situations which taught me that I do not have to attend every fight I'm invited to, not even the ones I inadvertently host.

And on the internet there will always, *always* be someone betting on you having a bad day so you get annoyed and distracted enough to get embroiled into arguing with them. I've been called out of my name and peaceful space even by those I share DNA with. Unfortunately for them, I have long since graduated with a first class in my 'use the internet like your last name is Knowles-Carter' degree. Although its name is a mouthful, the coursework is quite simple: only speak when you are sure you won't have to retract your statement.

Now, when it comes to situations that I am for sure have only been devised to see me publicly stumble or fall, I immediately go into silent mode. No matter how upset or worried something has made me (I'm only human so this is quite often), I no longer bring those negative feelings to the internet. There are times I feel like my vulnerability could be a helpful tool, but I've learned to reserve it for more long-form pieces of work like when I'm writing an article or a book. For my daily content, I've adopted a poker face which enables me to do my job and maintain a central sense of peace that appears impossible to disturb.

Any energy I do allocate to communicate with strangers

is strictly reserved for those whose support I believe to be genuine. If you show up to your place of work and ninety per cent of those around you support, champion and uplift you, then why on earth should the ten per cent get some shine? Not on my watch, sis. Not on my watch.

And yet, I know this isn't easy for everybody. I know of many people in the internet industry who have found themselves to be victims of unkind words on gossip forums or to be the continuous main character in a troll's story. I know of this because they understandably share how these false accusations, malicious abuse and unfiltered hate make them feel. All I want to do is drive to their home and unplug their Wi-Fi. These faceless leeches feed off the visual pain of others. And hopping on our phones to highlight how much they've upset our day does exactly what they want. It satisfies their desire to see that they have gotten under someone's skin. The thing is, not only is that hunger insatiable, it's grown more ravenous by having had a taste of what they like. I keep my fridge and cupboards empty of what they find delectable. Success and happiness are repulsive to them, so I share that in abundance and save the times when I'm not feeling so marvellous for myself. Some might say that this is disingenuous and that it would be better to share my life, warts and all. But having tried that, I firmly disagree.

Which brings me to another word that is crucial in the

social media repertoire: **authenticity**. Whilst it is very over-used, I struggle to find another word more fitting for what is now expected in regards to online influencers. Everyone wants to ensure that those influencers with wide reach and many eyes upon them are showing up as their most authentic selves. There are some downsides to this expectation, as that word has started to make content creators believe that if they aren't showing us their emotional haemorrhoids then they could be accused of lying. I have seen content creators share everything from their bank statements to details about their extramarital affairs, all in the name of 'transparency'. In a bid to appear as relatable and genuine as possible, they feel as though they owe their audiences ringside seats to everything going on in their lives. And because of this, there are many within those audiences who make it known that now they expect this level of 'intimacy', for reasons I can't quite understand.

To those who demand to see and know it all, I ask, firstly, why do you think you're owed a truth which doesn't impact on your life whatsoever, and secondly, once you know that truth, how does it enhance your life? We aren't entitled to more than people would like to share, and not respecting this means that the lines of privacy are blurred, and that's where trouble begins.

I know that intrusion of privacy all too well, because in

that last quarter of 2018, someone decided to share a video of a documentary where I proudly spoke about being a sex worker. This someone clearly hoped that they could sully my brand deals and ensure I would disappear forever. Now this revelation was no secret – it had been on television, for God's sake – but since having children, it wasn't a topic I wanted to discuss. I mean, no one was harmed during that period in my life – and actually, I think if you cared to run a survey, you would find it was the complete opposite – so why on earth was this being shared as information to try and tarnish me?

Because that's how it goes. If you attain a certain level of success, those who don't want to see you win are going to come out guns blazing. Listening to my manager's tearful voice, I was delirious with anger and sadness, more towards myself than anyone else. I had known this day would come, and unfortunately I had failed to follow my number one rule: hang out your own dirty laundry before someone tries to hang it for you. In an industry as cutthroat as this one, the only thing that ever wins is honesty, which gets you ahead of anyone thinking they have one up on you.

But it was too late. Now we were here.

I remember sitting on the edge of my bed, wailing. A scream so full of anger that Esmé came running into my room.

'Mummy! What's wrong?' she shouted, bewildered by my distress.

'Nothing, nothing,' I lied, quickly wiping the tears from my eyes.

I had always encouraged people to own every part of themselves, to turn their adversity into their advantage. But now I was petrified of having to walk the talk. What did this mean for me? My family? My career? Although I seemed to be surrounded by forward-thinking people, when it came to the idea of an ex-sex worker now being the face of a nuclear family, could they manage it? Only time would tell.

Later that night, I finally talked online about being a sex worker, and the reaction was one of such overwhelming support that I made up my mind then and there to never ever be in a situation where I would be forced to talk about something ever again. Especially if it only quenches the thirst of those who have not yet learned that their time is better spent picking up a new hobby they can then profit from, instead of engaging in gossip that doesn't propel them forward. To have been cornered into talking about a period of my life I hadn't even spoken about with my therapist felt like a complete violation.

After this experience of being stripped bare, it became crystal clear that the internet would always want to take more than it gave, and if I wasn't careful, it would always win. Moving forward, I had to rethink how I used the space.

I admit, I had tangoed. In earlier days, in a wild, desperate bid to win over the adoration of strangers, I found myself sharing far too much, especially when it came to my kids. When it comes to sharing children on the internet, not only is it very clear now where I stand, but I stand there with pride. Building a family brand has helped me give my children a lifestyle that I would not have been able to attain in this lifetime. And whilst I respect Kris Jenner, there is only so far I will go when it comes to allowing my children to appear in adverts. Esmé, who is my eldest, is now becoming more vocal with regards to her boundaries, and I am only too glad to respect them. Any opportunity that comes our way is always discussed with her in detail and if she's not feeling it, we let it go. It's never that deep.

I am also acutely aware of how my life and the work I do has an impact on my children when it comes to their relationship with social media. But does this choice mean that I should be willing to accept online bullying? Of course not. I have often said that I don't think it is taken seriously until someone decides to take their own life. With a heavy heart, I predict that irreversible erasure of these forums – which seem to attract hordes of faceless commentators who seek to unravel and intrude on the lives of those who share clips of their day on the internet – won't be victorious until the worst does happen. I think only then will these rightful campaigns which are fighting to have sites like these permanently removed, be taken seriously. I also think it will set the pace for how we seek to manage a world our children already view as the norm. I am part of the last generation who can remember what it was like to safely play outside or have to wait until your schoolmates were actually at home so you could call them. These days, two-year-olds know more about the latest iPhone than their grandparents ever will.

The gap in the understanding of technology and living a life online is astounding. A 2019 survey conducted by Harris Poll and LEGO found that one third of children between eight and twelve years of age aspired to either be a vlogger or a YouTuber, and there have been many other surveys which reveal similar data. Whether we like it or not, children now see sharing their lives, recording their hobbies or reviewing video games as a respectful and rewarding career path. Considering the fact that the highest earner on YouTube in 2019 was eight-year-old Ryan Kaji, who reportedly made 26 million dollars that financial year, I think it's safe to say that the data speaks for itself. As a parent who went to school in a time where the only place I had access to the internet was in the library, to now having children who go to schools where iPads are considered a necessity for them to complete their curriculum, I have to admit that I think a creative career where you can be your own boss is really going to be more children's first choice in the future. And let's be honest, my children already have a head start.

As contradictory as it sounds, however, I did have some hesitations when Esmé suggested she start her own YouTube channel, on which she would review video games.

'Ah, Esmé, I'm not too sure about that,' I said, hoping she would drop this subject and return to it on a day when I had thought of a stronger rebuttal.

'Mum, come on, that's not fair! You work on your phone, on Instagram. I want to build my own stuff too!'

I had to hide my smile. I liked how she referred to it as building her own stuff. And so, weeks later, I relented, allowing her to have a private YouTube account, which I control. The other condition was that she had to learn how to use a DSLR camera and a tripod and show me she was invested in learning how to edit her own videos. Because I wasn't going to do it for her.

Much to my delight, she is more excited about the filming and editing process than the nineteen views she has. Watching her get to grips with this hobby whilst also learning about things like internet safety and consent really made me feel like we found a way to not only grant her wish but strengthen her skill set in the process. This is something I would have been more inclined to say no to if I wasn't gravely aware of all the potential pitfalls.

Although I understand the moral confusion that arises when people speak about children featuring in their parents' online platforms, I must say, prior to my career becoming what it is, apart from the obvious – like blurring out the school badge on that 'adorable' back-to-school first day photo and never uploading images where they are even semi-naked – I had never given it much thought. The reality was that if including my first child in online campaigns meant the difference between being able to feed her or not, then there wasn't much to think about at all. Only now, after years of working with brands to help them promote everything from diapers to deodorant, do I really feel that I can finally be more selective. It is only now I feel financially well enough to be able to either suggest to a brand that my children don't need to feature in my content, or flat-out refuse.

Five years ago, both my brain and bank balance were in no such place. When speaking with a plethora of parents who do the same thing, it becomes clear that they feel tremendously judged for choosing this career as a way to either help supplement their living costs or keep them afloat. It's easy to sit in a Range Rover and make idle chit-chat of how the girl taking the bus should be living her life. Now that I've been in both the bus and the Range, I know it's not my place to thrust my moral compass on anyone. Everyone is just trying to better their and their family's lives. As long as no one is getting hurt, I've always thought best to leave them to it.

In a nutshell, I think if you enter this online world with a strong awareness of self, a plan and the understanding that you may always have to expand and contract your boundaries, I think what there is to gain from social media is limitless. I don't hesitate to admit how helpful it has been at helping me carve out a career which allows me to do things like write this book you're currently holding. For those of you who have struggled to gain access to various different workplaces or career fields, social media can act as your golden ticket to one day not having to ask anyone's permission at all.

It's also a great way to have a voice. In the past those under the spotlight of mainstream media had to go through traditional channels in order to have their say. Now the combination of smartphones and social media means that everyone has a mic and a soapbox. When used positively and without the intention of spreading misinformation, this can be used to life-changing effect. And even if you have no desire to grow an audience nor communicate anything to the masses, one can't deny how pivotal social media has been in recent times. Long after the communal online gathering after my father's demise, we find ourselves in universal collective mourning with regards to the world we perhaps took for granted pre-Covid. Even though we were all affected by the immediate change in our day-to-day routines at best, and by watching our loved ones fall sick or being sick ourselves at worst, the one thing we could all agree on is how vital social media has been during this pandemic. It has allowed us to connect, reach out, and even at times made us laugh when we thought we had forgotten how to.

Personally, the last year has taught me that I get the best out of social media when I remember to use *it*, instead of allowing it to use me. Thankfully, my days of refreshing my feed of choice are long behind me. I am very strict about the amount of time I dedicate to it, especially because I am able to see it as a tool that supports my business and not my business in its entirety. I have to remind myself daily that *having* a presence on social media is very different to always *being* present on social media. Most of my posts are scheduled in advance, my PA and management have access to my accounts, and I very rarely spend time scrolling.

Just before deciding to make these changes, I did suffer from imposter syndrome. There was a part of me that thought, 'Who do you think you are? Don't forget how much social media does for you, how much this audience does for you.' Whilst I would never want to overlook how beneficial the support of my followers is, I also think it would be disrespectful to my talents and hard work to suggest that I only have the career I have because of the people who engage with me, positively or otherwise. The reality is that the latter crops up more often than not, and if I continued to use social media the way I did five or ten years ago, then I might not have a career to speak of, because I most definitely would have asked someone to drop their location already so we could hash out whatever they disliked about me face to face.

Constantly being tempted to rise to the bait is exhausting, so my new boundaries ensure that I don't see the good or bad. I post and go. And it has been extremely liberating.

When I think back to that bespectacled, awkward teen who first set up a Face-Pic account, I don't think she had any idea just how much this new way of doing things was going to change her life. And you know what, even with its downsides, I wouldn't change a thing. But I'm glad I'm wiser now.

What I wish I'd known:

- Become best friends with the block button! My rules around why I block people aren't rigid. It could be as obvious as someone sending me a racial slur, to me just catching the faceless profile of a new follower that makes me feel uneasy. Your social media space is your internet home and you are within your rights to protect it how you see fit.

- Think before you tweet! Or speak. It's very hard to erase anything from the World Wide Web. If in doubt, wait it out, or at the very least run it by a friend who could perhaps offer some insight into how your words will be received.
- Don't become a slave to the algorithm. There is no way to please something you can't control, so share things that first and foremost make you feel good, that are helpful, practical or uplifting. Forever chasing likes or followers is a race that will never end and you will be the first to tire, so stay in your lane and do things your way.
- Know that you cannot please everybody. As your social space begins to grow, so will the dislike for you. Give those who want to bring you down or call you out *no airtime*. Because they thrive off drama and acknowledgement.
- Having a social media presence isn't the same as being present on social media. It may get to a point where someone else can run your social feeds for you. Embrace it.
- Have a plan. No one should aim to be an influencer forever. Remember to be clear about what you seek to gain from social media before it ends up taking everything from you.

Lesson 5

EVERY MICKLE MEK AH MUCKLE
– ON MONEY

Before we dive too deep, off the top I think it is important from a personal and legal standpoint that I remind you that I'm not a financial advisor, nor am I CFP certified. You're looking at someone who, until fairly recently, was amazingly comfortable not knowing what my earnings were. I was comfortable not knowing my credit score. I was comfortable with pushing debt collection letters that were never ever opened to the bottom of the drawer. And I grew far too knowledgeable about what time banks' payments cleared so that I wouldn't have to suffer hunger pangs again at work the next day.

Now, more to my surprise than anyone else's, I am someone who actively engages with her finances every single day. In order to really share what I've learned thus far about money and what it can do for me, I've had to think about my past relationship with it, what those experiences were rooted in and what I've sought to change along the way. I have even begun to assemble a team of people who help me understand why it's important to check in on my finances, no matter my earnings.

I can still remember the first time money made an impact on me.

Standing under the sweltering New York City sun, my great uncle Fitzgerald produced a crisp twenty-dollar bill, pressed it into my five-year-old palm and, gesturing to the store behind him, encouraged me to go in and buy something that would make me happy. I skipped off with his wife and my nan in tow and half an hour later we left the cool relief of the air-conditioned shop, with me clutching a bag and crying my eyes out.

'Candie! What's wrong, girl? What did they do to you?' He laughed, pointing at my nan and auntie.

'It's not them, Uncle Fitz! It's just that . . . I don't have any more money left!' I wailed, unable to control my sobbing.

The adults broke out into a chorus of laughter.

'Well, girl, that's how it is!' Uncle Fitz exclaimed. 'You get a bit of money, and then you have to spend it. That's the way life goes.'

'Well, I don't like life!' I cried, shoving my damp face into his neatly pressed white polo shirt, which he would always wear with matching tennis shorts.

Later that day, he would explain the concepts of working hard to earn money, not spending it all in one go and saving some for a rainy day. But in that moment he placated me with a large ice cream. Beyond this lesson from Uncle Fitzgerald, hearing school friends talk about pocket money and listening to Dad insist I return with the correct change whenever I ran an errand for him at the corner shop, there were no more lessons about what money was supposed to do for me. In fact, I had become accustomed to thinking that the only reason money existed was so that you could catch it to give to others.

Let me tell you about the barrel. For a long time, this cylindrical container was taller than me. To be able to peek at the bounty within, I would have to climb on a nearby ottoman and just pray that I did not tumble in. Inside, there would be soap powder, sugar, nappies, Carnation milk, deodorant, crackers and tea bags. Honestly, the inside of this treasure chest looked like what you'd find in a shopping trolley at the end of a supermarket sweep.

Taking up most of the space on what was already a small landing, the barrel would sit there until it was full. When it was finally time to put a lid on it, a man with a van was called, and then two adults would artfully (but not without bickering) get that barrel down the stairs and out of the front door. I often wondered as a little girl why they didn't just put the damn thing downstairs, and pack it there and then, but I did not dare make such a suggestion. This was grown-folk business.

The point of the barrel was to send groceries and toiletries back home. By the time I was an adult, I cottoned on to the fact that it wasn't just flour and – ironically – sugar being sent from Great Britain back to the West Indies, but it was money too, usually via Western Union. Western Union was constantly advertised on radio stations like Choice FM, which I listened to all the time as a teenager. And Western Union were not the only ones promoting the idea that money should be and was perhaps better off being sent backwards, not forwards.

'It's just how it is,' elders would tell me when I asked questions about it. 'You have to do good and make sure you can provide for your older relatives later in life. You are eighteen now; time to pay up, nothing doesn't come for free.'

What frightened me was that there seemed to be no pushback on this. Within our culture, it seemed to be an accepted, unchallenged fact of life. You knew as soon as you had a bit of spare change in your pocket, you not only had to account for the deductions for things like National Insurance and the tax man, you also had to account for 'hand back' tax – at least that's how I referred to it.

Naturally, I do think there are upsides to this habit. If you're contributing to the household in which you live because you're living rent-free at your parents', it makes sense you give back in some way. The problem is, things can escalate quite rapidly. What could begin as a £200 monthly contribution out of a £1,000 pay cheque can quickly spiral into £500 regular payments. Where I was raised, young people were being asked to pay up so much money at such a young age that they figured not only would they have more freedom if they left home, they would also be financially better off. I still have to hide the shock, shame and jealousy that usually overwhelm me when I hear that a friend of a friend was able to live at home rent-free in order to save up for a deposit on their first home. Because where I am from, that shit reads like a fairy tale.

If you happened to read my first book, *I Am Not Your Baby Mother*, you would know that money – or rather my community's lack of education about money – is something that has been a major bugbear of mine for many years. I know I'm not alone in thinking that this lacklustre education in money management, combined with the crippling financial expectations placed upon young black people, is grossly unfair, because whenever I have this conversation on a public platform, my inbox is flooded with other black people who feel the same way; they just don't feel confident enough to say it. With a little trepidation, I will also say I do think it is why so many other communities seem to be able to retain and spread wealth. I have noticed a plethora of other racial groups who have decided to do things a little differently. Instead of asking their children to chip in towards building a 'family' home back in their native land, they are instead committed to providing a financial springboard for their offspring, be that through savings, property, trusts or a combination of all three. In this scenario, the parents are making their children's lives easier, not expecting it to be the other way around.

Unfortunately, I am far too used to hearing tales from young people who have been told that the necessities that were required to raise them are luxuries. That they shouldn't feel entitled to things such as food and shelter, and they should most definitely prepare themselves for being turned over to the world the second the clock strikes midnight on their eighteenth birthday, now that they are adults.

Questions were not encouraged. Everything was on a need-to-know basis and unless you could contribute to those bills, then there was nothing else to discuss. And even when you could make a financial offering, it was always much preferred if you did not try to find out what the money was for or where it was going, especially not the money from Christmas or birthday cards which magically disappeared. As far as the elders in most households were concerned, if you were grown enough to ask questions, then you were also grown enough to find somewhere else to live.

By the time I was born, my mother and father had parted ways. I had been lucky enough to be ushered into a world of abundance. Upon my mother announcing she had fallen pregnant with me, my maternal grandfather – who was away in New York – had been so overjoyed that within the week, a barrel very similar to the one I would struggle to peep into as a child had arrived stuffed to the brim with nappies, baby clothes and a tub of baby-powder-scented petroleum jelly so huge that I was able to use that same product for the first six months of my own daughter's life to keep nappy rash at bay. Being my mother and father's only child and everyone's first grandchild, I wanted for nothing. My maternal grandparents took me on two holidays a year, I never had a chance to grow out of a school uniform and whilst I didn't get everything I wanted, I never felt as though I couldn't ask.

Things changed significantly when I was about eight years old. A tough change in living circumstances meant that for the first time ever, I knew what it was to feel hungry and to have to just suck it up. Witnessing the impact of my mother's divorce – she had to sell her home – I learned not to bother her about things like clothes and pocket money for lingering and labrishing with my bredrins in Piccadilly on a Friday evening. There was never enough cash for either. And yet I still lived a dual life, because visiting my father's home on the weekends was quite a different experience indeed. There,

I had my own room and the liberty of watching cable TV all day. The fridge was always so full that I would open it with caution, knowing that a Petits Filous pot or a packet of my father's favourite Parma ham could tumble down on me at any moment. There, I did not have to worry about things like turning off the lights or hand-washing clothes. For a whole forty-eight hours, it felt as if I were a child again, free of the stresses and strains that are part and parcel of a life peppered with financial woes.

Looking back, I'm sure my father noticed it too. I moved home so often after my mother had to sell our house that it became a little joke of his to always double-check where he would be dropping me off on Sundays after I'd stayed with him. And my sadness about leaving was mirrored by his frustration that we couldn't stay put for reasons I could never tell him because it would have meant betraying my mother.

But in his own small way, without intruding or making me feel as if I had to divulge family secrets, he found a way to be supportive. It is perhaps why he would weigh me down with bags full of food and snacks at the end of each weekend, always reminding me to share with my half-siblings. As I got a little older, the Christmas and birthday presents were less of the kind made in China and more featuring the Queen's face. He would tell me to buy myself some new clothes with that money or indulge in the things many of my peers were able to partake in more frequently than me. And I think it is why he gave me my first 'proper' job when I was fifteen, at that law firm where he worked in North London.

This meant that three times a week, instead of kicking about with my friends after school, I would have to power-walk to Selhurst station to make sure I got to Camden Town in time to relieve the cantankerous Jamaican receptionist who was in his mid fifties, and so seemed to have a pass for telling people exactly what he thought of them, especially if you kept him waiting.

'Wow, you're like the only one of us who works. That must be great,' a friend observed one day after I said I would not be able to join them in the dance studio for practice after school.

'Yeah, it is,' I lied, readjusting my bag and standing up straighter in the hope it would make me appear more mature.

The truth was, it was far from great. I was not heading to work for a cute internship that was devised to give me early insight into how the real world operated. I went to work because I had to.

Even at fifteen it was made clear to me that if I wanted or required any extras, I would have to go about securing them myself. There wasn't much spare cash to spend on my fickle teenage desires. And, speaking of school, it was at this specific one – the BRIT School – that I really began to understand how much I didn't have. An institution famous for churning out international pop stars, respected actors and bestselling authors meant that the environment was an incredibly competitive one. In a bid to encourage students to be as creative and carefree as possible, there was no requirement to wear a school uniform. Never before had I understood the importance of looking the same amongst young teenagers. All of a sudden, I went from a school where you only saw labels once a year on mufti day, to seeing fifteen-year-olds turning up with designer handbags and earlobes weighed down by gold and diamond earrings. I became hyperaware of the fact that the bulk of my clothing was from stalls at Tooting Bec and East Street markets, and my footwear was never of the season.

'Oh, shit!' I yelled one morning when I realised that the snap I had just heard was due to the entire weight of my body coming down on the glasses I so desperately needed.

'Candice, watch your language!' I heard my mum yell as I began to cry.

I cried because I knew what I would have to do. Not wanting to add to her ever-increasing financial burden, I found some tape and stuck the broken arm back onto the frame, and that's how I went to school until my mother could afford to buy me new ones. To my surprise, she was willing to supplement making the change from glasses to contact lenses. Whilst I was so grateful, I knew coins for luxuries like these were few and far between, and I also knew it would be up to me to pay for future lenses. The part-time job my dad had found for me would help with that, with all of it. So no, I was not going to work to seem grown-up. I was hustling because I had no other choice.

My grandparents had come to this country and followed the rules. They kept their heads down, worked hard and didn't step on anyone's toes. Money from pardners had ensured that they were able to move from a one-room home (note that I said one room, not one bedroom) where they had to share the bathroom and outside toilet with the rest of the tenants, to a three-bedroom home with a garden. They had savings and pensions, and it seemed to work out OK for them – but for their own children, not so much.

This meant that by design, most of their grandchildren would never know what it was to be financially stable. It's a complicated matter. As I've gotten older and taken the time to teach myself the fundamentals of wealth, and how to create wealth to pass on to future generations, one thing that comes up time and again are the opposing schools of thought when it comes to the matter of credit.

At one end of the spectrum, I remember elders comparing the use of credit to doing a dance with the devil.

'No, sah! Mi nah inna dat credit ting deya. If mi cayan't save fi it, my cayan't have it.'

And they meant it. They did not care how frequently credit card companies wrote to them; those letters would go straight in the bin, even though that very week they would go to Sackville Travel in Brixton and put a deposit down for their next trip back to their Caribbean homes. Every Saturday, like clockwork, they would head down to that travel agent and pay fifty pounds at a time until that holiday was paid up. They never stopped to think that the credit they were offered could have paid for the holiday in one go, and then all they would have had to do was pay back the credit card company with the same dedication they paid the travel agent.

At the other end, I also remember being around people who thought credit was pretend money they could spend as they wished, with no consequences.

'By the time they get their money back, I'll be dead. At the end of the day, these companies know what I have and don't have. So, them offering it to me when I'm already broke is their poor choice. Not mine.'

Usually those who saw credit as the ultimate financial enemy did not need it. They either already had enough money to be considered comfortable, or they were lucky to have enough to cover their rent, one round of drinks for the colleagues they didn't like and an ill-fitting outfit bought online. These people would never understand why others had to be indebted in order to make ends meet.

I cannot wholeheartedly say that I disagreed with all those people. Of course it made sense to live within your means, budget and put money away for a rainy day. But the problem was I had felt hunger pangs on days where the sun was so hot and high it was like the concrete had turned to slush. So when the opportunity to have money did arrive, I couldn't care less if it was cash, credit, cheque or debit. I was all 'show me the money', as my dad used to say like Cuba Gooding Jr in *Jerry Maguire* as he waited for the cashpoint to dispense his pound notes.

I was definitely one of those who saw credit as something to play with. And speaking from experience, those folk were usually both cash-desperate and supremely uneducated about the extent to which the use of credit impacted their credit scores, therefore potentially ruining every big financial decision they tried to make in the future. But that was it: they did not believe in a good future, period, let alone a financial one. As far as they were concerned, it was going to take God himself to bust through the clouds and present them with buckets of gold for them to live the life of their dreams. And they believed that – or anything close to it – was unlikely to happen. So, what do you do when you already think that this is your lot? That this is as good as it gets?

Let me tell you.

A little like that five-year-old who spent that entire

twenty-dollar bill in one go, spending everything I had was a trend that would continue well into adulthood. It wasn't helped by the mentality that I was spending pretend money rather than the real deal every time I used my credit card. I still remember the faint bubble of excitement I felt when a credit card company first wrote to me. In that moment I felt special. They had even pre-approved me for a credit limit of £200, which seems like an awful lot when you're used to going through the spare change tin.

Because I was so in the dark about how it worked, I had no idea that I was not special at all. I was just a young kid with a clean credit history; I was their dream. And it did not help that the advice handed down to me by my credit loving elders was to take them up on every offer to its highest limit. I would spend as close as possible to the limit, too. Not just on nonsense like fast fashion and make-up, but also on necessities like lunch and toiletries. When I was nearing the limit on one card, I would just sign up for another. Of course, I knew that at some point I would have to pay the money back but, in the moment, it all felt so easy and quick. And when I was not racking up credit card debt, I was living in my overdraft. None of this felt unusual for me. When you come from a place where everyone does not have much, you don't see these financial choices as anything more than what had to be done.

Because my credit history was still unmarked and in its infancy, the needs of the household also became my responsibility, and it was hard to say no to them. Before I knew it, I had cable contracts, payday loans and even sofas in my name, as the only adult in the home with good enough credit. Life don't come for free. I kept telling myself it would be OK. I was always employed; I had no choice but to be. So, when the letters started to arrive, I began to try and balance all the minimum payments. Sometimes I would pay a little of an overdraft with the cash I withdrew on a credit card, knowing that the next month I would quite literally pay through the ass for that. But all around me, these short-term solutions made sense.

They were better than the long-term solution, at any rate, which was the popular idea that smart women, lucky women, beautiful women, should just marry rich. Because as far as the common conversation was concerned, if you make too much money, a man would not want you anyhow, as that was going to seriously dent his ego.

Once, I told an older family member that I had finally decided to call it quits with my then white boyfriend because to him I wasn't a girlfriend at all, I was just the black girl he was fucking. He couldn't possibly take me home for dinner; no one in his village would be able to understand what had 'gotten into him'.

'Oh, don't mind that,' she encouraged. 'He is from good stock, try and make it work. You don't want to end up with a poor man – or worse still, with a man who will be annoyed if you decide to make a better life for yourself. Better to settle with someone who is already made.'

I decided against spelling out the clear racism and just let her ramble on. There was no use. She was part of a group of people who would encourage a girl to protect her virginity rather than her credit score.

Whilst on paper it seemed the easier thing to do, I had been around women who stayed with rich men just because it took the pressure off them. Though on the surface they seemed to enjoy the trappings of what their husbands' take-home allowed them to buy, those things didn't keep their pillows dry at night when they were left wondering where said husband was.

This approach to financial stability collectively under-mined the hard work and innovative ways of thinking I saw in black women all around me. When having to think about financial role models within my community, I must note they were all female. Whilst now you have to be on the Forbes 30 Under 30 in order to be considered successful, back then it was all a lot simpler, a lot more grassroots. Left and right, black women were making moves with their money-making ways. There was June with her hair salon, Pat with her cake business, Sandra running a childminding service, 'Auntie' Sarah working every hour God sent to get her children into better accommodation. I mean, everywhere I turned, black women were on their hustle.

But I wasn't there yet.

I can still remember the heat of shame that fell over me when I first went into a pawnshop alone. It smelt of stale tobacco, Charlie body spray and tough choices. This was not my first foray into peeping into this world – I had often accompanied both adults and mates there when times got tough. But now I was the adult, and because of all the pretend money I had blown, my lack of financial nous and the need to get the bus to work, I scraped together all the gold from the bottom of my broken jewellery box and made my way to the local pawnshop.

I could barely make eye contact with the woman who spoke in a tone so low it sounded more like a grumble. She reminded me of my primary school secretary – all harsh bottle blonde in desperate need of a retouch and with a chest so heavy one would think she might topple forward each time she stood up. But there was also a jarring warmth bubbling beneath her haggard exterior.

'That will get you, about . . . thirty quid, babe,' she said, looking at me with eyes filled with more care than judgement.

I knew that what I was handing over to her was worth perhaps three times that, but I was desperate.

'That's OK, thanks,' I sighed, trying to find a flicker of joy in the fact that that money should be enough to get me through to next payday.

Stepping out of the dim shop back into the brightness of the day really made me realise just how much that space swallowed all the light, and the hope that comes with it.

Suddenly, I heard someone call my name. I recognised the voice instantly.

'Candie girllllll!'

It was Samson.

I gritted my teeth. I hated the way he called me Candie. I know he meant no harm, but it really did annoy me.

Samson was just one of those figures in the community that could do no wrong. A wheeler-dealer from a large, well-known family, he would do anything for anyone in a heartbeat. But he was also a busybody and wanted to know everyone's business. He stopped his bike abruptly next to me.

Great.

Great. Great. Great.

I took a deep breath and put on my best at-ease expression.

'Hey, Candie girl, how are you?' He smiled. If you could call it that. You see, Samson had no teeth at all. Well, perhaps a few at the back, but I had never seen them. So when his cheeks did rise in that way they do when someone smiles, it was just bare gum on show.

'Oh, hi, Samson! I'm good, you know. Just looking for a piece of jewellery for a friend's birthday,' I hastily lied. I was trying to close that gap that nosy black folk fall into and prise open if you let them.

The way he squinted at me let me know that I had been rumbled, but he played along.

'Yes, man, you haffi hail up those who support us on their birthdays,' he replied, laughing. 'Tell your fam I said hello, yeah?' he called into the wind behind him as he flung one leg over his rusty pushbike and pedalled off with my half-hearted response licking his back.

I sulked off, promising myself that with my next pay cheque I would sort everything out and finally get my act together, but of course that didn't happen. A year or so later, I was working in admin in a hospital. A friend of mine was able to get me the job and back then, nine pounds per hour was something. It was also great because I got paid weekly. I had done the maths that if I just snagged some extra shifts on top of my 7am–2pm job, then I would be good. And boy, was I looking for some variety. Whilst I was glad to be making money, I don't think I've cried so much when on my way to work before. I worked in the basement of St Thomas' Hospital; it was so deep underground that even the morgue saw more activity than we did. The room smelt old, and any desire for ventilation was mocked by the fact that there were no windows.

It was my job to log all the electrical faults that occurred in the entire hospital. And trust me, there were a lot. From a theatre reporting that a few lights had blown to a ward complaining their TV was acting up, to even more pressing matters like people being stuck in a lift – all of that had to come through me. And once I had logged these jobs, I then somehow had to try and chase the guys whose role it was to fix things. These men were white, usually in their late forties, read *The Sun* and lived on a diet of bacon sarnies and beige-coloured tea. So, as you could perhaps imagine, a young black girl essentially asking them if they'd done anything but stare at Page Three all day never went down well. Their eyes would glaze over me as if I were less than nothing. And then they would speak over my head to my supervisor who, aside from being female, was like them in every way.

By the time I arrived at work at 6.45am every morning, there would be at least one hundred dockets on my desk which had come through overnight. And there I would sit, processing and chasing until 2pm, when I could finally leave because I had learned early on to forsake my lunch hour. I only persevered because that kind of money was a rarity and I figured staying there would help me get a handle on all these debts.

But every time I went to pay off my overdraft, credit cards or finally get my jewellery back, a fresh bill would drop. It was a never-ending cycle. I had to make sure I had enough money for gas, or electricity, or food, or the internet before it was cut off yet again. Those things always took priority. So, when the letters demanding what I owed started to arrive, I buried my head deep in the sand. One day they would get sick of writing and calling, I said to myself.

I often thought about asking people for help during that time, especially from my father, but my pride wouldn't allow it. I was caught between wanting to admit that I was financially struggling but also thinking he had eyes in his head so he could see that for himself. The way he had acted when I was younger had shown me that he did notice that when it came to finances, his life and my life were vastly different. Nothing had changed. He knew it and so did I. And by this point something in our relationship had shifted. I often thought that he would ignore certain things not to spite me but those around me. It's a funny one, but in that moment, I would have rather gone hungry than admit how hard it was.

What I always wondered was, why couldn't others understand that whatever that person had, they could work to have, too? I think it's because, where I'm from, there is a lingering sense of scarcity. There is a misconception that we cannot all be financially solvent at any given time. At best there can be a maximum of two people in any one family who can assume the position of having flexible purse strings. It does not help that this misconception is supported by facts. The wealth gap between black people and their white counterparts continues to grow wider. As reported by the *Guardian* in June 2020*, data showed that 'typically, black households face the biggest deficit. Compared with white households they have lower earnings and less cash in private pensions, investments or other assets to draw on'. This is not shocking to me in the slightest. Even back then I knew more about the inner workings of the Job Centre than I did about stocks and bonds. There were times when I was out of a job and the only option was to go and sign on. Unfortunately, this was a common experience amongst my friendship group at the time.

'Mate, the wickedest ting is bare of us are smarter than the people talking down to us in there, you know?' one friend fumed after yet another episode of being made to feel small in the Job Centre.

'I know,' I sighed.

---

* Hilary Osborne, *Guardian*, 'Financial inequality: the ethnicity gap in pay, wealth and property', 20 June 2020

For the first time in forever, I was annoyed with myself for not having gone to university. Perhaps getting drunk and half-assing my way to a 2:1 in something like English Literature would have given me more options. But even my friends who had photos of themselves in their cap and gown on their mothers' faux fireplaces were on zero-hour contracts in soul-sucking call centres. So, I quickly shoved that regret to the back of my mind with the same haste I was shoving away debt letters in the bottom of the drawer.

They seemed to be ever-increasing. They had started calling, too, so I changed my number. The fact they couldn't reach me didn't mean I felt any better. But from what I could see, the dull headache that debt created was something that I would have to learn to live with. All around me, people had gotten used to having to rob Peter to pay Paul. Even though this was not a life I wanted for myself, I could not see any way out. At best, I would get a decent job and work my way up the ladder, then I would be able to pay off my debts. That was my plan.

They do say life laughs at our plans.

Moving out of home came with zero fanfare for me. It was simply what I had to do, to jump-start my own life. Everyone around me had become far too comfortable with the idea that I was always going to put myself last and I could foresee that I was going to end up alone and angry. So, packing one suitcase and deciding to try and build a life for myself didn't scare me at all. In my eyes, outside was the warmer of two cold worlds. And as much as I can now make peace with that young girl who had no right making that leap, in that moment, like so many who had made that choice before me, I would figure it out once I was out in the world.

I was already used to paying my way, so moving out gave me no financial shock, but I was blown away by how now there never seemed to be enough money to close the gaps. Most jobs available to me were minimum wage and maximum hustle. It felt as though I would need a miracle to make enough money to live, pay debt and, dare I say it, enjoy my life.

And then there was parenthood. In the midst of becoming a mother, I went into survival mode. Grand plans of saving money and chipping away at overdue payday loans became the last thing on my to-do list. It was all about keeping the kid fed and dry.

The next time I really had to think about the mess I had made, there was a lot more to lose.

'Is there something you want to tell me?' Bode's nostrils flared with anger.

'Err . . . no,' I said sheepishly, whilst trying to think about what I could have done to annoy him.

'OK, well, let me tell you. The letting agency have run a

credit check against your name and it has come up saying you have a CCJ. A county court judgement, Candice. The landlord now wants nothing to do with us.'

I swallowed hard. Oh, shit. In that moment, I didn't really know what that meant. But I did know it was bad.

We were trying to move from our tiny two-bed flat in Croydon to a more spacious three-bed home in Milton Keynes, and my growing belly with our second child only reinforced our sense of urgency. With truly little money in the bank, we were trying to make this move happen on borrowed money and a prayer, but it was clear the prayer had been returned to sender. My past had caught up with me. I felt vulnerable and stripped naked. In that moment I understood why most people thought it was bad manners to discuss money. They must have felt like me. I could not imagine a billionaire feeling this way.

As per usual, instead of allowing that pain to show, I decided to throw a verbal jab.

'Oh, please. Don't act like you've always made smart moves,' I shot back, rolling my eyes. 'Plus, if it weren't for my stepdad helping us out, we wouldn't be able to pull this off anyway. Let's just find another house and chill.'

Even though my defences were up, I wanted to self-combust. The debts had come back to haunt me in a spectacular fashion. Me reminding Bode that it was the kindness of my stepfather that was enabling us to move was a blow so low, even I knew it had been unnecessary; but in that moment it was the only way I could deal with my embarrassment.

Luckily, Bode is like a dog with a bone, and after many phone calls and promises, we were able to retain the landlord's attention – but it came at a cost. We would have to provide him three months' worth of rent instead of six weeks'. This threw our calculations way off by almost a grand. But it was money we would have to find if we wanted to move.

Credit to Bode, because he made it happen. But speaking of credit, once the deposit was secured, that was next in the order of business.

'Do you even know what your credit score is?' Bode pressed weeks later, as we were bubble-wrapping fragile items to be packed away.

'No!' I insisted, screwing up my face. 'Only people with money need to know those things. I know I don't have that, so why would I bother checking?'

'Because you want to know how it can be fixed. And you need to remember this is not about just you any more, Candice. That CCJ impacted us all. You don't want that to happen ever again.'

I knew he was right, but I was uncomfortable with the emotions speaking about money brought to the surface for me. It made me feel out of my depth and childlike. I had assigned myself to a life of financial lack and whilst I was OK with thinking like that in private, it annoyed me that now he knew that too.

'Listen,' said Bode. 'I'm not perfect. And it will probably take me ten years to pay off all my debts, but the most important thing is bringing all of that into the light, that way you can get an idea on how to handle it.'

That was the first time I had ever heard a dire financial situation being discussed as something that could be changed for the better instead of referenced as something that was a foregone conclusion.

A few months later when we were settling into the new place, we finally took what I think was one of our most romantic steps ever: we were honest with each other about our debts. At this point, I think I need to enlighten my sisters about GVM. 'Get Vex Money', as it's often referred to (or also sometimes called a fuck-off fund), is the money most women in my community are encouraged to have regardless of their current relationship status. It can be used for a plethora of things, but as the name suggests, it's the money you should have on you or underneath your bed just in case a situation has vexed you so much that you need to make a hasty exit. For example, when I was younger, whenever I said I was heading to see friends or going on a date, everyone from friends to male family members would ask me if I had my GVM on me, just in case.

As a mother, I can appreciate the safety net that GVM provides in a young person's early social interactions. To be on a date or at a party you want to leave but cannot as you don't have enough money on you can at best be a terrible inconvenience and at worst the difference between you making it home safely or not.

My issue with GVM is when it's specifically spoken about as the money every woman in a serious relationship should have that their other half does not know about in case she needs to walk out. Which is partly why I had never really told Bode everything. Put simply, where I came from, it was encouraged not to reveal all your financial cards to your partner.

Personally, I am on the fence about GVM. Whilst the astute feminist in me believes it can be a very necessary and powerful tool, the optimist in me can't help but think that sometimes even the mention of GVM dilutes the honesty and open dialogue that should be present in every relationship. In more plain-speaking terms, I do wonder: if there is a true need to squirrel money away to exit a relationship, why be in it in the first place? This isn't to say that I don't see the benefits of being financially stable enough to live a life free of abuse or a relationship that impacts one's mental health.

But maybe our desire to retain GVM isn't about the money at all, but the fact our intuition may be suggesting we are with someone we cannot trust. Now, I don't have GVM but I do have personal savings that Bode knows about. For me, that's the best of both worlds. But earlier on in our relationship, being honest about finances was a struggle.

Admittedly, it took me a long time to get to the point of opening my proverbial purse to show there was in fact nothing but lint lingering within it. Whilst this perhaps wouldn't have been a problem if I had no interest in Bode's pay packet at all, the unfairness of it arose when it became clear that I felt I had a right to know every pound and penny that came his way whilst simultaneously remaining mute about my own dosh. The necessity of secrecy only began to intensify as I found myself in the position of making more money than him.

As that idea became a reality, I became even more tight-lipped about what I was earning. I had to retain my GVM at all costs. I was conditioned to think that at any moment this man was going to stitch me up, so better to keep my money to myself.

And that worked . . . until it did not.

Not only is the process of buying a home with someone the closest I've come to re-enacting the earlier days of having lost a loved one when it came to the level of stress that we dealt with, it is also the most revealing task I've ever agreed to undertake. Having to provide all my financial information in black and white felt far more intrusive than when I had to talk about how much debt I was in. It has taken me years to understand that a huge part of my discomfort was down to the fact that I was always encouraged to hide something from a man. Although this perhaps makes more sense in the earlier days of dating, considering the fact that he had – not once, but twice – held a pillow to my abdomen whilst I was taking my first shit after a C-section, I can't help but recognise the smoke and mirrors of it all felt very unnecessary.

Still, long before house buying was on the cards, when we finally had The Talk about our debts, Bode was far more forthcoming than I was. And with reason. He had been employed by the same company for almost half a decade and was slowly working his way up the career – and therefore financial – ladder. Even if things would be tight, he did not have massive gaps in his work history like I did. He would figure it out. I, on the other hand, was now almost two kids deep with a CV so peppered with holes that it resembled Swiss cheese. Although I knew in my heart my less than ordinary work path meant that I had a wide variety of skills, these were not immediately going to help me clear out my debt. The weight of it all felt crushing.

Sheepishly, I went to my side table where I had been

putting those debt letters I had collected over the years. Every place I had ever called home, these letters had come with me, but this was their first time since being sent to me that they had seen any kind of light. It honestly felt very freeing to finally be able to not only share this information with someone else, but most importantly, confront myself and feel supported in doing so. Since leaving London, I had really begun to be honest about the kind of life I desired and being haunted by debt did not feature in the future I had planned for myself.

With Bode's encouragement, I researched and downloaded apps which revealed my credit score. Whilst I knew I was in a bad place financially, seeing the actual figure was chilling. Sixty-seven out of a possible seven hundred. The app reinforced its concern for me by showing the words VERY POOR in stern caps, just to ensure that I had gotten the message.

Message received.

'See, that's not going to work if we are ever to buy a house one day,' Bode warned gently whilst looking over my shoulder.

I sighed. He would just never shut up about buying a home. As far as I was concerned, that was folklore. You did not get to be a homeowner unless you were lucky enough to buy your crib in 1901, or you inherited the bricks or some bucks to buy them. Of course, there was also the rarity of your parents being able to gift you the deposit.

'I dunno.' I shrugged. 'I think it's best we just make this place a home.'

OK, so it was technically my landlord's place, but not only is long-term renting nothing to be ashamed of, it was also the norm for me. Unfortunately, when many of my friends were able to get their parents to write them a letter which allowed them to be classed as homeless by their local council, I had no such luck with mine. The argument was, why would I want to leave a perfectly good home? It pained me to see friends and even some family members be offered a space of their own at a more affordable rate.

Which is partly why, years later, when I had a little family in rented accommodation we could afford, I wanted to allow myself to just be. This seemed to be the pinnacle. Whilst I wouldn't admit it to Bode, I was only willing to work on clearing my debt so that I wouldn't feel haunted by it, not because I was hoping to ever hop on the property ladder. Plus, even though we were still in the red because we had chosen to move again, we were now beginning to be able to breathe a little more when it came to our finances. Whilst we were nervous about having another mouth to feed, we were not as skint as when we had Esmé. There was always a little more left to play with at the end of the month, most of which

I would now use to chip away at my debt. As big a task as it seemed, I just committed to taking the smallest of steps.

And sis, let me tell you, it's funny how quickly things can change when you think they can.

Less than a year later, I ran down the stairs to the kitchen. With each step, I wanted to squeal with excitement, but I didn't want to wake the baby.

'Boooooodayyyyyyyyyyyyyyyyyy!' I yelled once I was safely out of earshot of the baby's room.

Bode pretended to jump as if he had seen a ghost.

'Ah! Ah!' he shouted in his deep Nigerian accent. 'What is it that has you this excited now?' he asked. 'Share the news!'

'Oh, nothing,' I lied, spinning around just like my secondary school dance teacher had shown me.

But then I couldn't pretend any further.

'I just wanted to see your face when I told you that not only can I pay off my final personal loan today, but I can also pay the remainder of the loan my stepfather stood guarantor for so that we could move.'

I squealed, unable to play it cool.

'You what?' he asked, his tone heavy with disbelief. I didn't blame him. I myself had run through the figures three times before really believing it.

'Baby, I did it! I did it! I am down to my last loan! And with the gig I just got paid for, I've done the maths and I can also pay off that loan you took out so we could move the first time,' I repeated, reaching up and grabbing his shoulders. I slightly shook him so he would know it was real.

'Oh my God,' he whispered, allowing the weight of his body to be held up by the kitchen counter worktop.

I could see that he wanted to cry. And admittedly, so did I. It was one thing to finally be able to look forward to not fearing the postman or turning my phone over in an embarrassed haste if my debt collector phoned me in public, but it felt tremendous to now help clear up the debt Bode had taken on for us when we had no other choice. Even though we had left the flat that we required that loan for, we had been sure to keep up with the repayments because my then stepfather had been our guarantor, even when those close to him advised him not to do so. I had watched Bode get up early in the morning of every payday since we had been together and pay bills with a smile on his face, even when he was left with less than £100 to last him the month. To be able to take this off his plate now not only felt good to do for him, but for myself too. I had finally regained faith in myself when it came to making and managing my money. After years of feeling like I was in a financial black hole, I was finally able to come up for some air.

As romantic as it would be to end on that note, I do not

want to tell half a story. Because even though I could now call myself debt-free, that didn't mean that I could just wipe the slate clean. The poor decisions of my youth would haunt me for a little longer yet – seven years, to be exact. And that would be a pinch we would both have to feel.

It all started with a dream, a dream I deemed as so unachievable that draping it in humour was the only way I could reckon with it.

'You know what, Bode, let's see what we would have to do to be able to buy a home a few years from now,' I said, laughing, one insignificant afternoon.

He slowly slowly spun the office chair around.

'Really?' he questioned.

'Yeah, sure! I think it would be good to get an idea of what we need to work towards.'

Things had once again changed and this time they had changed so much that for some reason dreams that I once thought were always out of reach no longer seemed so far-fetched. Sure, I had no hopes about family being able to chip in and my bank balance was not in current agreement with my plans, but I just had a feeling that I couldn't shake.

And so, he asked.

A few days later, once we had put the kids to bed, he revealed something he had been thinking about all day.

'How would you feel if I told you that, according to the

mortgage broker, we would be able to buy a house now?' he asked, his full lips trying hard to stifle a smile.

I drew a sharp intake of breath.

'Now?' I swallowed. 'Now, now? I was thinking more three to five years down the line.'

This wasn't what I had planned at all. Bode could sense my confusion and fear.

'Babe, come on. Let's try,' he encouraged.

And so, we did. Although yet again our lack of financial understanding still had one more blow to give.

'So, even though we've cleared off our debts, our credit scores still indicate us as people you shouldn't trust with credit. Therefore, there isn't a high street lender in the land who is prepared to lend us the money. We are going to have to go with a lender who doesn't mind working with high-risk people. Of course, this comes at a cost.' Bode sighed as he explained the ins and outs of the call he had with the broker a few days later.

'Oh, for fuck's sake,' I moaned in response. 'Does the penalisation ever end?'

'What we could potentially do is go with it and in a year or two, we can then transfer the mortgage to a high street lender.'

'Fine,' I said, kissing my teeth.

But it felt like the repercussions would never end. I wanted to go back to that eighteen-year-old and slap every credit card out of her hand. I wanted to go back and pay every bill on time. But it was too late. I would simply have to wait for the effects of all those things combined to run their course.

Two years on, I can confidently say the repercussions of my stupid financial choices have finally stopped haunting me. For the first time in my life, I not only have money saved but I have multiple credit cards that I only use to help boost my credit score. I'm the co-owner of a very lucrative business and Bode and I are making plans to buy our second property and become landlords ourselves.

But most importantly, I've learned to invest in educating myself about money management and what financial steps I need to take so that my children never look at money as something confusing or complex, but as something that, when used correctly, can help them and their children continue the path to building generational wealth. I hope to offer them more blessings than burdens, and provide a life for them which, though it doesn't wrap them in cotton wool, allows them to be children for as long as possible. I want them to respect not only cash in hand but also have a deep understanding about how each financial decision can later impact their lives. As I was often told, nothing don't come for free, and the fee of learning the hard way when it comes to money isn't a cost I would want them to pay.

What I wish I'd known:

- It is not your duty to sacrifice your financial well-being because of peer pressure or archaic traditions. Think long and hard before using your credit or standing as guarantor for someone else's financial commitments.
- There is a lot school didn't teach us about finances, so the best way forward is to self-educate. There are many books, financial platforms and online tools which will teach you how best to manage your money.
- Good credit is worth more than money in hand. Try not to use credit cards or apply for payday loans unless you can clearly see how you are going to pay it back. Even then the latter should only be used in a dire emergency.
- Credit is not the devil, poor use of it is.
- Don't feel ashamed to say when an outfit or outing is outside of your current budget. Keeping up with the Joneses is an expensive habit.
- There is no such thing as failed financial future. With patience, hard work and consistency you can turn your financial life around.

Lesson 6

THE WOO-WOO –
ON MANIFESTATION

If I had a pound for every time someone asked me about 'manifesting', I wouldn't need to energy-cleanse my crystals under a new moon or write down my intentions weekly any more. I would have all the money I needed to buy every desire my heart required and then some. But luckily, I love talking about this. This version of self-help changed my life in such a spectacular fashion that I have no doubt that the 2013 version of Candice would have walked right past the current one, never thinking she would be leading this life. And that, my sistas and sisters, is down to learning all these lessons I'm sharing in this book, but also to the power of the woo-woo. Of that, I am convinced.

Perhaps it's because as I'm writing this during the pandemic we're living in the upside down, or maybe it's because the vast number of corrupted politicians and contrived policies remind us that hell is a lot closer than we think, but manifestation – or 'big magic', 'positive thinking', 'the secret' or whatever you want to call it – is enjoying a bigger moment than those totally useless but oh-so chic petite Jacquemus' Chiquito bags. Whenever I speak or write about using LOA (the law of attraction for the woo-woo newbies) my comment section, direct messages and emails all simultaneously go nuclear. Because no matter who or where you are, the idea of improving your life in a spiritual way is very appealing. I have found most people only truly get on board with the notion of energies or the universe having their back when they are promptly out of the former and have run out of human connections to do the latter. To put it bluntly, most people only pay attention to this way of thinking when they are flat on their face.

I know that was true for me, because prior to being flat on my face, I was not curious enough to open my mind to this kind of thing.

In fact, I did not find manifestation, it found me. When I first found a copy of *The Secret* knocking about in a family member's home, I was enthralled. The concept of it was so straightforward and easy, a five-year-old would have got it: your thoughts control the universe, so if you want something, all you need to do is put that thought into the atmosphere and then go about living your life as if you've already achieved said thing and it will come to you. It was like a revelation to me. I remember my first manifestation project. I worked relentlessly on manifesting a white feather. My dad had just died, and for some reason I felt like feathers were little signs from him that everything would be OK. Later that day I saw a feather so dirty, it looked grey. Upon reflection, it was probably a rogue one from a pigeon, but I took that as confirmation that not only had my manifestation worked, but also that everything really *would* be OK. I never glanced at *The Secret* again because I thought I had it down. Little did I know, I was wrong across the board.

The years that followed were mercilessly shit. There was setback after setback, personal problems, and don't get me started on issues with the opposite sex (as you'll find out in the rest of this book). Life was abysmal. By the time the ideas around manifestation came back into my life, I was a mother. Granted, I was with Bode, a man I loved, and by the skin of my teeth turning up every day to a job as a marketing assistant in a publishing house which I quite liked, but there was still the feeling of wading through treacle. Everything felt difficult. In my head, I was at constant war with myself, and the physical spaces I inhabited felt like a battleground. I was deeply unhappy with the woman I could foresee myself becoming (pessimistic, bitter and jealous) and I knew my daughter deserved to see a more well-rounded version of me.

I had enough of those negative female role models to last both our lifetimes; I didn't want that tension to stay on repeat.

I can't remember what came first: the idea to quit my job – one I had quite literally fought for – or picking up *The Secret* again. Whichever it was, what was now blatantly clear was that I could *think* about having something all I wanted. But if I wasn't taking *proactive steps* alongside that thinking, it was tantamount to having a car with no petrol in the tank. Both my dreams and I were going to be stagnant.

So the first thing I did was hand in my resignation. The reality was that whilst it was a good job in publishing that many people my age would have been desperate for, it wasn't the stuff that set me on fire. Working in marketing really confirmed to me that I didn't want to sit in on meetings about what an author's cover should look like, because I wanted to be the author. I didn't want to brainstorm ways in which we could align with an author's personal brand, I wanted to build a brand of my own. And most importantly, I didn't want to have to report to a boss, I wanted to be my own boss.

Becoming clear about what I wanted was another import-ant step. There could be no half-assing it. And because of that, I knew there was only one thing I could do to prove to the universe that I wasn't interested in anything but building my own career and brand. I would have to show a massive leap of faith, and for me that was going all in on designing the life I wanted. I would actually never recommend this to anyone, because it wasn't easy. It was almost exactly three years after quitting that job before I ever saw a cheque for my efforts. *Three years.*

I've read everything there is to read on the LOA, manifestation and the universe. One thing that annoys me is how most of these books and articles seem to skip the part where the people that they make these promises to are more than likely going to be dead broke, lacking in motivation, with their back against the ropes, thinking, 'What the hell have I done?' I always like to warn people that if they truly want to activate their magic, it's going to go pitch-black before they see a speck of light, and I ask, 'Are you prepared for that?' I also add that there is no timeline nor deadline to how long it will stay dark for – you just have to have resolute, unwavering faith that once you're through that tunnel, the light will be so blinding you will have to wear sunglasses even when in the shower. There are some people who would rightfully argue, 'Well, if the universe has my back so much, why does it need to go dark in the first place?' To that I say this: 'Have you ever done a hard reset on your phone whilst it's still on?' Exactly.

So what's really happening here is a hard reset on how you've been taught to think about things. And when you really open yourself up to the many ways we have all been preprogrammed into thinking and behaving, it can be very overwhelming. As a society, we have been encouraged to think that there is a lack of everything. A lack of time, money, love, beauty. Whatever you can think of right now, just throw the word lack in front of it and you get the picture. Rewiring your brain and trying to make it believe that not only is there enough of everything for everyone, there is actually an abundance of all resources in both the physical and spiritual form, is going to be one of the hardest jobs you will ever do.

Because it is, in fact, a job. I started to understand that the reason this way of living didn't work for me the first time was because my actions were akin to taking one driving lesson and expecting to pass my test the next day. I was realising that this mental maintenance, this continuous checking of my thoughts and feelings, was going to be a full-time job. It would be exhausting, but I would never retire from it because it is necessary.

When I began to track what my first thought or emotion was when a less than perfect situation arose, I was horrified to find that eighty per cent of the time, I led with something negative.

'This is terrible.'

'I hate it.'

'Why can't I be better?'

As this awakening was made more and more clear to me, it became obvious that I would need to flip the narrative.

The voice in my head, the one that decided there wouldn't be a cookie left for me before my hand had even reached for the biscuit tin, would have to get used to me thinking positively. So conditioned was I to only heed to negative internal chat – with all the self-doubt, fear, misunderstanding and self-flagellation that came with it – that when it came time to actively pay attention and change my thought process, it was a struggle.

But ever so slightly, I began to see changes. Slowly but surely, I worked on not always leading with the worst-case scenario or getting down on myself if something went wrong. I did something which I felt was quite radical: I started to believe that the universe, God, the energy – whatever you want to call it – was actually committed to ensuring that things worked in my favour. The more I thought that way, the more a passage of ease would present itself. There would still be times I stumbled because I was hardwired to believe that good things couldn't happen for women like me, but I kept working at it. I also struggled to accept that I was worthy of a joyful, largely stress-free life.

I think there were numerous factors at play here. The first was inexplicably linked yet again to the community from which I came, and how I was accordingly raised. Sista, you know what I'm talking about.

'You have to be twice as good to succeed!'

'Get used to always being offered the scraps.'

'Be grateful to even have a job. Just put your head down and work hard.'

This 'yes, sir, no, sir, three bags full, sir' type mentality really runs amok in the space I'm from. I don't begrudge it because in many ways, thinking like this is what has kept us alive. Remaining compliant and making ourselves small was often key to us literally living to see another day.

So, as I was learning from *The Secret* that I didn't need to work my fingers to the bone to be successful, or that trauma isn't necessary to make my life better or make me more deserving of positive outcomes, I was often resistant. Surely this couldn't be true? Surely it couldn't be as simple as my mindset standing between myself and the things I wanted, because let's be real, if it were that easy, many more people would be only too happy to wake up on Monday morning. For me, something wasn't adding up.

This is a good moment to talk briefly about religion. I was raised as Christian by grandparents who had come from the Seventh-Day Adventist background. When I was younger I went to primarily white churches, whose version of praise and worship was a tambourine, coloured ribbons on sticks, and a white-robe-wearing choir of which I was a silently unwilling participant. I paid attention in Sunday school and waited politely whilst my grandparents gossiped with other churchgoers once the service was over. As I got older, I ventured out and found churches of my own to attend. They had a little more 'spice', as the young people would say. The voices of the choirs were definitely blessed, the message was always spoken passionately, and someone was always delivered.

But what I also noticed was that many of the things the Bible asks of us most of the congregation couldn't manage. Instead, in true human fashion, people seemed to pick the parts of the Bible that supported their interests and personalities and would dance around the rest. One of the biggest examples of this, in my personal opinion, was the difference in the standard of living between many of the pastors and those they were speaking to.

Every other Sunday (I won't lie and say I attended each week), I would watch as a preacher decked out in an eight-piece suit (nine if he was wearing a toupee) would take to the pulpit and remind us that it was tithe and offering time. Depending on how much time he had, he would recite lyrics about how the size of your offering would reflect the size of your blessing, and if you really wanted that new house or for your child to get into that university, or for the good Lord to zap that cancer out of you, then you sure as hell better put your money where your prayer was. Then the bucket would pass around, and those who only had a few pennies to spare would place their hands right to the bottom of the bucket, so that you wouldn't know they weren't dropping fat pound coins, which always made a heavier, thudding noise. The arrival of card machines in the church made this process a little less awkward.

As soon as the service was over, off the pastor would ride in a car that looked like a bullet-proof Bentley, whilst waving at the very same members of the congregation who had started to walk home, unable to afford public transport. Their bus fare had long since made haste with the pastor. And if you didn't get the new house, or your child didn't make it to university, or you still had cancer? Well, as the pastor explained, 'Even if God doesn't make good on his promise in this lifetime, he will make good on it in heaven. Let us rejoice and praise Him.'

Now hold up, wait a minute, rewind, selecta.

You mean to tell me that these people, myself included, were giving their last, having to accept that the pain and suffering we were currently experiencing might go on forever as we know it, and whilst it was going on forever, we were supposed to rejoice and revel in it? Oh no, honey child, this cannot be.

So when it seemed that I was finally able to make the LOA work for me, alongside being amazed, I was also very fucked off.

Did other black folks know this? Did they understand

that the power we thought could only be bestowed on us by our boss, our significant other, even our pastors, was already readily available within? Now, being able to create this space for yourself doesn't automatically mean that there still aren't other universal hurdles like racism, sexism and all the other -isms in between. But the cool thing with this is that when the energy says 'it doesn't see colour' or something of that ilk (which often feels like a cop-out when said by others), this thing actually means it. For about three months, therefore, I relentlessly shouted about how accessing this level of yourself was the most life-changing tool you could ever be blessed with, and guess what? You didn't need to put your bus fare in a bucket to get it.

My advice wasn't met with the excitement I expected.

'You stay there, that sounds like voodoo to me.'

'Please, girl, whatever I can manifest for myself, the Lord can do better.'

'Are you on drugs?'

As much as I tried to explain that changing the way I thought didn't mean that I was totally ruling out the idea that there was a larger force that could help us, no one wanted to get on board with the belief that the first port of call was a strength that was inside them.

Somewhere in my mind, this revelation made me feel as though this is how it must be to be white. You wake up in the morning, free from the weight of the world's stereotypes and microaggressions. You make your coffee not worrying if today is the day the police will assault or kill you. You take your whole self to work because no limb nor pound of flesh will be considered too different, too black, too strange. And most importantly, no matter the circumstances you were born into, you always take for granted that the world was built to tip in your favour.

I often see a meme which never fails to make me chuckle. It says:

Maybe you manifested it.
Maybe it's your white privilege.

The meme speaks to my soul because in the last few years especially, manifestation, tarot reading, meditation, yoga, crystal work – everything that could possibly be tied to the practice of the LOA – has had a serious Goop moment. To show how I myself cannot escape the advertising of big magic, let's talk about the fact that I was only today-years-old when I learned that white sage, which is often used to cleanse bad energy from spaces, is not only part of an important religious ritual called 'smudging' (burning herbs) for indigenous people, but as recently as 1978, it was illegal for Natives to actually practise their religion within the United States. Yet in desperate times, I have found myself purchasing 'smudge kits' from white women running online businesses for 'spiritual awakening', many of whom I doubt know the roots of the practice from which they profit. Now am I saying that white people shouldn't use all the tools available to help them introduce the law of attraction in their lives? No. Am I saying they need to thoroughly educate themselves on where these practices derive from? Bingo. Because these items – like so many things that were taken from communities who were, and in many ways still continue to be, deemed as outliers – get repackaged and sold at a level that means those who can claim it as their heritage are now priced out of the very thing they and their ancestors fought to preserve as their own.

Because Gwyneth did say she popularised yoga, right? LOL.

That is all I ask that we be mindful of. White people will most definitely have a jump-start in regards to making the LOA attraction work for them because our society already does a really good job of that. But if you are not white, it can work for you too. I was gobsmacked by how, all of a sudden, the things I thought were proper hurdles just didn't seem to be blockers for me. I always got the job (after years of convincing myself of the many reasons why I wouldn't), I built a loving family (after years of chasing men who only loved themselves) and most importantly, I really started to believe that things wouldn't end how they had begun (after spending decades listening to others telling me not to have high expectations).

So, I thought I would share some of the tools I use to help you get there too, and to remind you – and me – that things don't have to be the way others have decided they will be for you.

SETTING THE RIGHT INTENTIONS

I have learned the hard way that before I sit down to even put pen to paper, it is important that I am crystal clear about not only what I desire, but also what my intentions behind such desires are for the greater good. It is my great belief that the **why** is more important than the **when**. I have found the universe to respond very well to the intention of sharing blessings, be they wealth or wisdom. It's better to desire millions of pounds to better the lives of those I love than to wish for new shoes and handbags for my wardrobe. Whenever I haven't led with the best intentions, my shit has been popped down for one reason or another. This isn't to say that you can't think of satisfying or saving yourself, but usually when that is the primary reason for engaging with the universe, there is only so much magic you can attract.

VISION BOARDS

Seeing is believing! Whenever I get down on myself, I remember everything, absolutely everything, began as an idea, a mere thought, a shooting star dancing across the darkness of someone's mind. Knowing that, I think it's very important that there is a physical representation of what you would like to achieve which you can refer to multiple times a day. This is what's known as a vision board. The good news is that the need to collect all your old magazines and get busy with Pritt Stick and scissors has long gone. Don't get me wrong, there is something so grounding, almost meditative, when it comes to the old-school ways, but technology has given us better tools for doing things. There are apps specifically made to create vision boards and to bookmark things that make your insides tingle. I have found that it is very effective as long as you make a point of returning to it regularly.

THE POWER OF PLANNING AHEAD

My grandad often used to tell me that the pen is mightier than the sword. There is a reason why the most successful people tend to write things down on paper: there is something about doing so which really feels like you are cementing a thought or a plan.

The year I'm writing this is 2020, and I don't think we need to fact-check what a shitshow that was. But what would you say if I told you that – apart from those literary events which I was supposed to attend in the big wide world, all of which got cancelled – every single plan I had for myself unfolded in a way that meant 2020 had the greatest positive influence on my life.

You see, each new year I dedicate at least eight hours (spread over two or three days) to writing out – by hand – a meticulous plan for the year ahead. I use a template with the same title every time. What I love most about this framework is that it makes you think and write about the year just gone. In fact, I would say this specific outline makes you spend more time reflecting on the last 365 days than focusing on what has not yet come to pass. The first year I did this, it made me realise that even the hardest moments, during which I was drowning in my own tears, turned into diving boards for good later on in the year.

Another thing I do, at the beginning of each year – both the common calendar and the financial one – is specific to the financial aspects of the LOA: I write cheques to myself. I can't take credit for this trick. I actually watched a video where the actor Jim Carrey described writing a ten-million-dollar cheque to himself before landing his first major lead role. The first year I tried it, I was vague about what my financial asks were. But still I found a chequebook for an old bank account and I wrote myself numerous cheques. Not only did I write down specific amounts, but I also signed them from companies that would give them. Once done, I folded them up and tucked them in my purse.

Over the course of the year, I was shocked to find that every single cheque found a way to manifest itself in the physical world. Since then, I have made it a habit to routinely check in on my cheques and make sure that my intention behind my financial requests isn't compromised. As previously expressed, coming from a background that preached hard work above all else, this practice was one of the most difficult for me because it seemed a little too easy. As far as I knew, making money was always hard and if someone's fingers weren't calloused, you probably wanted to question that person's work ethic. Now I know nothing could be further from the truth. This isn't to say I don't have hard days, but I've learned that making a living from doing not only what I love, but I'm very blessed at, is actually not a daily grind at all.

GRATITUDE LISTS

I use gratitude lists in a slightly different way. Where most people use them for things they're thankful for that have happened in the past, eighty per cent of what's on my gratitude lists are for things that haven't happened yet. For example, I've already expressed thanks for another year of great health. Our forever home. Oh, and my new teeth. Currently, I'm sat in my first home which I love but now realise isn't our forever home, I'm healthy but I know I could be fitter, and I still instinctively cover my mouth when I laugh. However, it's all good because I really know the power of a gratitude list written from the perspective of the future.

A few months ago, a wonderful professional organiser by the name of Dilly came to help me sort out my clothes. She persuaded me to part with the things I no longer loved and whisked them away so they could be resold. A few days later, a woman sent me a picture of one of my gratitude lists – it was stuffed in a pocket of one of my old dresses she had purchased on a fashion resale website. Reading it quickly, I had to fight back tears. Every single thing on that list had found a way to manifest itself into my life. I couldn't believe it. She offered to send the list back to me, but I knew it had fulfilled its purpose.

Never underestimate the power of already being grateful for things you can't yet see. Speaking of seeing . . .

FEELING BEFORE SEEING

In my opinion, this step is by far one of if not *the most important*, but it's often overlooked. When it comes to creating your dream life – be that to do with a career, a family, money, whatever it is you desire – you have to be able to replicate the emotions you would feel if you already had this thing in your possession. For example, trying to manifest a pay rise but being led by how you feel because you're still in your overdraft right now is not exactly ideal. Think about the things you will do once you do get that pay rise and, within your current limitations, do them! Perhaps you can't buy that new handbag yet, but you sure as hell can go and try it on in the store. Hell, take pictures of yourself wearing it whilst you're at it!

In other words, within reason, try and do physical things which will trick your mind into enjoying the emotional experience that will come if your desires become a reality. From personal experience, I've found that one of the strongest things I can do is create an almost sensory attachment to whatever it is I wish for.

For example, as you know from Lesson 5, wanting to buy a home was very unlike me, at first. As Bode likes to remind me, in the earlier days of our relationship, I would harp on about how home ownership was not something I saw myself being able to do, ever. But I was riding a woo-woo high, so when I asked him to call a mortgage broker just to see what we would have to do in order to buy a home, say in the next three to five years, I was taken aback to find that actually it could happen in less than half the time. And so then I was all in.

I cannot describe the stress. On the face of it, all the chips were stacked against us. Poor credit history? Check. Fewer than two years of accounts as self-employed? Check. Not enough for a deposit? Hell, I wished someone would run us a cheque!

But still, I held onto the fact that the LOA cares not for logic, and so I worked on feeling as though a house I had spotted on the internet in the town we wanted, and that I loved, was already mine. I watched videos showing the layout on repeat, making notes of where all our current furniture would fit. I made sure to 'check in' on our home at different times during the day, just to make sure things were all in order. When we made our offer, I even sent myself a 'Congratulations on your new home!' card to the new address, really cementing the belief that the only one who could open the card was me, and this was weeks before we had even closed on the deal. All of these things made my body replicate positive, happy emotions that I was sure I would feel once we heard the house was actually ours.

Less than a month later, when I pushed the key into the door of our new home, the first thing to catch my eye was the card I had already sent to myself.

CRYSTALS

Once I learned that crystals weren't just some colourful stones that caught dust on a mantelpiece, the game was really on. Just like with *The Secret*, I stumbled across a book that broke down in non-woo-woo terms not only what crystals could help you achieve, but from what part of the earth the more popular ones come from. I have found them very effective in keeping my mind balanced in times of stress and anxiety, using them as a focal point during meditation or simply tucking a few in my bra (yes, my bra! I've often been changing on set or in a changing room where I'm only reminded of their existence when the time comes to free Betty and boo, and a handful of crystals come crashing down to the floor) for a sense of extra spiritual protection and support.

I use citrine to help support my financial manifestations by keeping a piece of it in my purse. I usually have obsidian in a pocket when I'm stepping into unknown territory or I know I may have to spend time with someone who doesn't have my best interests at heart. And in my bra, I usually always tuck a piece of rose quartz. Keeping that 'love stone' near my heart is a gentle reminder that I should lead with love always. I know many would say that crystals perhaps provide a placebo effect and I'm OK with that. But I think anything that prompts the idea that all things work together for your good isn't a bad thing at all.

MEDITATION

I have benefitted so much from introducing meditation into my life that I often wonder why taking the time out to be still and centre yourself isn't in the national curriculum in all schools. Like most, I came to meditation with a mind that wouldn't quit yapping. The longer I sat there, the louder the thoughts became. Sometimes, I would get up from a fifteen-minute session feeling more mentally exhausted than when I first sat down. But, over time, my mind fell quieter and quieter until one day, there seemed to be no trace of any intruding thoughts at all.

In moments of intense stress or serious decision-making, I've been known to slip away from meetings for some time to meditate. Doing so allows me to return to situations with a clearer head, and I now honestly don't know what I would do without it.

If, like me, you find it too hard to just be still on your own volition, please may I suggest guided meditations. I find it really helpful to dip in and out of apps and YouTube videos to find them. I often read about people transcending, floating or accessing another dimension. The closest I've come to any of the above is having a feeling like a ringing sensation throughout my entire body; it literally feels as if I am vibrating.

TAROT READING

Ever since I was a young girl, I've had an affinity with those who were almost borderline obsessed with tarot readings. At least once a month, I would go with various members of my family to see a woman called Ann, who has long since died, bless her soul, who would read tarot cards for them.

As I grew up, I understood that tarot reading wasn't cool or trendy, and it was usually negatively linked to witchcraft and other untrue stereotypes. I've had various tarot readings over the years and perhaps I'm blessed, but I have to say many of my readings were spot on, one frighteningly so. Whilst I have no interest in learning to 'pull' cards for myself, I do genuinely believe that there are many who are very gifted at doing so for themselves and others.

One word of caution: I think tarot reading should support one's life and decision-making, and not the other way round. Life is full of twists and turns, most, if not all, of which are unavoidable, but I do think that in especially dark or confusing times, tarot readings can often be used like a lamp to illuminate what can't be seen.

*

So those are the practical tools, resources and things I do to help me access a more spiritual plane that helps me achieve what I want. But there is something I have to add, and I purposefully didn't mention this at the beginning because I wanted to give this more spiritual approach a fighting chance: really, and I mean *truly* committing to the LOA, big magic or *The Secret* is not the key to a worry-free, stress-free or problem-free life, because that would mean that your life has the potential to be perfect, and fortunately there is no such thing.

I say fortunately because upon reflection it's the moments that knocked me to the ground – like, taken the wind out of me, Muhammad Ali style – that have all, *all* turned out to be for the greater good. The key difference is, prior to believing that I was entitled to a life more full of rainbows than shitstorms, I found it very, very hard to bounce back after the downers because I was preprogrammed to believe that the only thing I could do in that moment was give up.

Now I see my life as a video game. There are myriad levels and opportunities, and an abundance of gold coins to catch. But just like a video game, the promotion to each level requires a new skill set, a new way of thinking, and maybe even the need to pair up with someone who will help me achieve my end goal. Now I use the LOA, I see that as a cheat sheet for the video game. There are no promises that this game will be free of baddies or challenges that may momentarily require me to hit pause and think about my next move, but it does mean that everything is rooting for me. It does mean that the odds are in my favour. And it does mean that I will win. And it is my true belief that you can win too.

What I wish I'd known:

- The LOA is not for a select few. Unlike when people say 'they don't see colour' or they 'aren't judging you', the LOA really, really means it.
- The first step is in the feeling. So much of how we think happens subconsciously, it can get tiring trying to manage that all day. So, one of the quickest hacks is feeling good. Finding ways to make yourself feel good supports the LOA no end.
- You can read all the material, watch all the movies and listen to all of the podcasts, but the only person who can commit to using the rules of the LOA is you.
- Start small! It's hard to go from being hardwired to thinking negatively about everything, to trying to manifest a holiday in Barbados. Start where you're at.
- People will write you off as crazy. And as your life starts to shift to reflect the kind of energy you're giving off, the gaps between yourself and many people you've known your whole life will grow wider and wider. You can't bring everyone with you.

Lesson 7

THE BLACKER THE BERRY – ON COLOURISM

I hadn't felt like this in a long time. Not quite a decade, but it had definitely been many years since I wanted to unzip myself, shuffle out of my skin, a bit like a snake, and leave behind this torturous dark overcoat. Perhaps I could crawl into a space where the depth of my blackness didn't bring with it such painful rejection. It would be a delight to only have to deal with the palavers that arise from simple, straightforward racism. I thought about what sweetness I could enjoy, just by existing on the right side of black, by not being this black.

I closed my eyes and imagined the thrill of appearing for a screen test or audition as palatable or exotic. I half smiled at the thought of someone asking, 'What are you mixed with?' because my skin afforded me the privilege of not appearing to be 'fully black'. I could be pretty. Not just pretty – or in my case 'quirky' – for a dark-skinned girl. See how it feels to be offered a job because the tone of my skin is more like those who work there. See how it feels to not be immediately labelled as angry, but perhaps feisty, instead. See how it feels for someone's eyes to linger on me a little longer, instead of looking through me, like I don't exist at all.

It was the feel of the hot tears beginning to seep through my false lashes that snapped me out of it. When I opened my eyes, my laptop screen had gone black, as black as me, so I was confronted with a truth I didn't want to own that day: I was still a dark-skinned black woman.

Like I said, it's not often that the low confidence which haunted me as a teen shows itself like this, but as with all things I'm working on, there are the moments I'm just triggered, innit. Earlier that afternoon, the five white faces staring back at me on the screen had looked as if they wished their broadband would start playing up at that very minute.

'Oh, for fuck's sake!' I spat. 'Come on! I've been working on a similar project for ages! We last spoke with them in December. Oh my fucking God.'

'I know, I know,' one shoulder-less face interjected.

'No, you don't!' I snapped. 'You have no idea how it feels to be looked over for things I've worked so hard for just because I'm dark-skinned.' I slapped my hand down on my kitchen table as a way to exorcise my anger.

For the third time in the last six months, I had seemingly lost an opportunity or been beaten to the finish line by a light-skinned woman. I was furious. Usually, I was very measured when it came to communicating the less than desirable systems within the black community, especially if those windows of weakness were left cracked so white people could peep through, but enough was enough.

For most of you reading this, the term colourism won't be new to you. You will understand it, see it at play, and you will know, although possibly not be able to admit, how much you benefit from it. There will be those of you who, like me, were perhaps made aware of colourism before racism, because it wasn't the fact you were black that encouraged prejudice, but instead how black you were that proved to be the problem.

Others of you will never have heard of the term colourism before, and your perplexed expression will be giving that away right now. So, let's start there, with the Oxford English Dictionary's definition of what colourism is:

Prejudice or discrimination against individuals with a dark skin tone, typically among people of the same ethnic or racial group.

Individuals with the dark skin tone like me who ended up being treated like shit across many columns on life's spreadsheet.

When I was a child, colourism didn't affect me. For at

least the first five years of my life, I was unaware that in the years to come, the tone of my skin was going to be a constant hurdle. I lived in a home with black people of all different shades and if there was ever a mere whisper that there was a hierarchy due to skin tone, that chatter never found its way to my ears.

But by the time I was a student at the first of two primary schools I attended, I had begun to notice that other kids were far friendlier to my lighter-skinned best friend than to me, although I couldn't find the correct language to describe what I was seeing. But still, outside of that playground, I didn't feel anything was wrong with me until the early days of secondary school. It was here that the opinion of the boys who went to the local same-sex school nearby became very apparent.

I remember trekking up to Crown Point with friends after school one day. Innocently enough I thought we were just going to get chicken and chips and knock about for a bit, but it seemed they had other plans. When we finally arrived at the top of the hill, there was a group of boys waiting.

The ringleaders of both sides made small talk, whilst the rest of the boys announced very loudly that they were going to rank the girls in terms of their prettiness, with the highest number being the ugliest and the lowest being the prettiest. My stomach grew tight as I knew what was about to happen; I wanted to leave but it was too late.

'Man, you gotta stop riding with the blick girls, man, you're too pretty for that,' the ringleader of the boys said to the leader of our pack whilst gesticulating towards myself and the other dark-skinned black girls. We had unconsciously gathered together as if doing so would make the shock of the inevitable assault any less painful. He had used a term I had heard countless times, but its edges were as sharp as ever.

Blick is a derogatory racial slur against a very dark-skinned black person.

Blick. Blick. Blick. It would come to be one of the most popular slurs thrown my way over the years.

I wanted so badly to point out that this boy was the same complexion as us; he too was dark-skinned. But I knew that would only make things worse. So, I stood there, having counted eleven girls and knowing what would come next.

'Yeah, this one,' the ringleader continued, pointing at me. 'She's deffo number eleven, bottom of the pile,' he confirmed, never even making eye contact with me. Then he proceeded to rate the others, of course giving the top spot to our ring-leader, who happened to be the lightest-skinned of all.

'It's mad cause, I know you're black, but you don't even look it. You could be a video girl.' He smiled at her.

That she could. The most popular video vixens of that time were light-skinned Latinas, mixed-race or very fair-skinned black women who could get away with being a mix of the two. Although I wasn't shocked that I was rated the lowest, with my very dark skin and the need to perm my hair to take the kink out, it still hurt. And as you will read later on in this book, this bias was a trend that continued well into adulthood. For years I was told that the tone of my skin, its deep cocoa hue, was grotesque and unacceptable, usually by those of the same race as me. And although it was in a far more subtle manner, society made it clear that it was in agreement and had been for quite some time.

Now, as ever, when we speak about the hierarchies we find ourselves to have unfortunately (well, for me, anyway) inherited, I think it's important to understand the historical context for them. So, let's do that for colourism. Before I proceed, there are, of course, books, papers and investigations dedicated to this topic, and none of what I'm about to write will be as cohesively communicated or vigorously investigated as what those bodies of work have to offer. As someone who has the dark-skinned end of this stick, my patience for the minutiae of how colourism came to be is about as thin as the skin of those who engage in the harmful practice of skin bleaching. But here's what I can express in the most basic of terms.

When slavery was legal, the slaves were divided into two camps: the house negro and the field negro. In fact, it was a different kind of N-word, but if you're a white person reading this, I don't ever want you to think you have a pass to say it. So, let's use our imaginations and continue to live life with our two front teeth still intact.

House negroes were almost always lighter in complexion. Their biological proximity to whiteness allowed them to catch a reprieve from toiling in the field under the hot sun by taking on the more domestic roles. Whereas by stark contrast (quite literally), field negroes – those who weren't able to feign racial ambiguity or didn't happen to possess features that made people think twice about their race – had to do the back-breaking field work. To add insult to injury, the masters of these plantations took great delight in watching the divide that this colourist regime had created consume the slaves. More often than not, they would encourage the house negro to use their 'Massa'-given power to abuse and/or belittle the field negro, adding to the already hot and hostile environment between the two.

And like most of the divisive tactics employed during slavery, this system, this hierarchy which is solely based on how closely one conforms to Eurocentric beauty standards, has found a way to seep into present day. You can see it when rappers jokingly rhyme about house negroes and field negroes, whilst not noticing the irony of having all of the racially ambiguous women gyrating in the background. Or you can see it when young black girls like me were almost always being put to the bottom of all the piles. Yep, colourism is still very much alive and kicking.

When I think back to TV, magazines, adverts and even music videos when I was growing up, being able to see a dark-skinned black woman playing the lead role in a show or on the cover of a magazine was a rarity. When it came to models, there were two – Naomi Campbell or Alek Wek. And to be honest, Wek's beauty was always up for 'debate' as she didn't possess the features that Naomi did. Funnily enough, when it came to music, there was a little more choice, with Lauryn Hill really leading the pack as a dark-skinned songstress the industry seemed to respect.

But the other women, most notably rappers, either had to erase their womanhood entirely and become 'one of the boys' (Missy Elliott) or be so committed to selling sex and sex alone it was a wonder record companies didn't just put a blow-up sex doll on album covers (Lil' Kim and Foxy Brown). The line was clear: songs about being a wife or mother, or soft and loveable and worthy of respect and protection were given to light-skinned artists, and racy rap lyrics about fellatio were as good as the dark-skinned artists were going to get. My dark-skinned friends and I often joke that the reason dark-skinned black female musicians are unable to penetrate the current mainstream market is because the powers that be still think we are indebted to them for allowing Lauryn

Hill to have the career that she did. I hope the fact that we have had to result to using humour to take the sting out of blatant colourism helps illustrate how insidious this issue is.

So, the media were in agreement that our depth of blackness wasn't palatable, and most people in and outside of our race made it clear that they weren't going to celebrate our beauty either, and there was nothing we could do about it.

Or so I thought.

I cannot remember where and how I came across bleaching creams. Actually 'come across' is the wrong expression, because bleaching creams, or 'toning agents' as they are sometimes referred to, are everywhere once you decide to pay attention. There was one particular brand which lurked in many a bathroom cabinet in various homes. Positioned as an ointment to help reduce dark scars and marks, most people I knew used it on their knees and elbows hoping to erase the extra build-up of blackness (the irony being that wanting to erase any part of blackness is a problem in itself) which can accumulate on those points of the body. It wasn't until I was in my early teens that I realised that many people used it and even stronger products to help take the colour out of the skin all over their body. And as luck would have it, I was coming of age at a time when skin bleaching was growing in popularity.

Between bashment songs such as 'Cake Soap' by Vybz

Kartel and skin bleaching agents now being readily available in almost every specialist black hair and beauty shop, it's not to say that my desire to be light-skinned was an impossible feat. I didn't have to venture far to find women who too had succumbed to the pull of bleaching creams that would help them transition from being dark-skinned to a 'beautiful browning', a change which would afford them the positives which we were both consciously and unconsciously told one could only acquire through being light-skinned. These women could usually be spotted a mile off, because for most, the products they had chosen to use didn't agree with them. Yes, they were lighter, but their skin was always blistered and red, not quite unlike sunburn. For those who could afford the continued expense of bleaching, those side effects were usually few and far between, but upon closer inspection, the dead giveaway was always the knuckles. For some reason the melanin in that space just didn't want to budge, so try as they might, the true hue of their skin was always visible on their body.

Not that this has stopped anyone – in fact, being able to maintain a stringent bleaching routine is seen as a way to show affluence in many communities. Because bending to the ideals of beauty laid out by Western society takes big bucks, and these products – which can come in the form of creams, tablets and even injections – aren't cheap. It's reported that in 2017, the global skin-lightening industry was worth 3.4 *billion* pounds and it is predicted to almost double by 2027. And these products aren't hard to come by, either. As previously mentioned in Lesson 1, those who owned hair shops which sold products predominantly for black people, to an overwhelmingly large, black customer base, never thought twice of trying to get you to add some skin bleaching agent to your shopping trolley.

'Want something for whitening, darling?' one stocky shopkeeper asked one day when all I was trying to do was buy some cocoa butter and scram.

'I'm good, thank you,' I replied, not returning his smile.

'Oh, come on now, it will make you so pretty, all the boys will like you,' he said, winking.

'I said I'm good,' I repeated, more firmly this time.

'Look at Shelly – Shelly, come show your skin! She uses it. Helps her stand out. Shelly!' he shouted once more, beckoning for a petite black woman to come forward.

'Yuh nuh hear she say she nah want di ting,' Shelly shot back, suspiciously jamming her fists into her bomber jacket pockets. But it was too late, I had already clocked the blindingly obvious: Shelly was a skin-bleaching addict. The ashy yellow tone of her skin and bulbous red blister where the product had quite literally burned her were clear signs of bleaching. I don't know why she thought hiding her hands would change anything.

'Thanks,' I muttered, trying not to look at her for too long.

With hindsight, I realised I didn't want to stare for two reasons. The first being, I didn't want it to come across as if I were judging her. There were no pride points to be gained in thinking that because I had somehow been able to ignore the pull of bleaching creams that this made me better than her. I had been her and, in more ways than one, felt the desire to be her as she painfully clung onto the idea of being someone else, someone greater. Someone afforded opportunities and kindness that the dark-skinned version of herself wasn't. But we were no longer in this together. I wasn't going to join her, and she made it clear she could no longer be with me. Being me came with more emotional pain than her bulbous, oozing blisters. We both knew that. We all knew that. And of course, there is data to support that.

University researchers Jill Viglione, Lance Hannon and Robert DeFina from Philadelphia[*] found that lighter-skinned female prisoners are sentenced to 'approximately 12% less time behind bars than dark-skinned inmates'. **And** there isn't even reprieve in the Home Office. A BBC investigation found that 'women with the darkest skin tone were four times

---

[*] Jill Viglione, Lance Hannon, and Robert DeFina, 2011. "The Impact of Light Skin on Prison Time for Black Female Offenders: A Research Note," *Social Science Journal* 48: 250–58.

more likely to have their photograph rejected than women with the lightest skin'.

Even before this data was available, we just knew. I think even in his reserved and awkward way, my dad tried to find ways to boost my confidence when it came to my skin tone. He never explicitly spoke with me about colourism – come to think of it, he wasn't explicit about much at all. But he did make it clear he thought my skin was an asset.

'Come, let me rub your face!' he would say.

'Dad, no! I told you already I'm not wearing any make-up!' I would giggle.

But still he would gently rub the outside of his hand along my cheek just to be sure.

'You're like Cadbury's chocolate, man! Jeez! Your skin is so pretty.'

Or when I was at his house and the six o'clock news came on, the whole street would know about it.

'Cand! Cand! Look, come, my girl is on! No one talk now! You know I love Charlene White. And look at her skin, Cand! Like yours! So smooth. I just love her, you know,' he would say, chuckling to himself.

Most importantly, his actions mirrored his words. Outside of my own mother, every love interest or celebrity crush of my father's could be considered a dark-skinned black woman. I never mentioned it, but seeing him appreciate a beauty similar to mine was perhaps the reason I learned to love the skin I was in and decide against using bleaching creams.

Seeing what were once rich-toned black women now having to flee from the sun come summertime, either by constantly using an umbrella or having to cover up their arms and legs entirely, left me feeling sad. Although I deeply understood the desire to wake up and live in a body that would offer me that sense of ease, the same sense of ease I was urgently searching for, I just wasn't able to do it to myself. Unless God Himself found a way to change me, I would die as dark, if not darker, than the day I was born. But this confidence, which has to be constantly worked on, didn't completely erase the societal pressures that continued to reiterate that light was right. And sometimes, society won.

Like the time a black man held the door open for a light-skinned black woman and as I walked a little faster so I too could take advantage of his gesture, he let it go, laughing and saying that I wasn't cute enough, just so that the message was received loud and clear. Respect and protection aren't entities that can exist alone. I don't protect spiders because I don't respect them. The lives of black men aren't protected by the law because they aren't respected by the law. And the same applies here. Colourism has enabled us to watch darker-skinned black women not be respected and therefore not protected, and it seems like the only ones who care are the ones quite literally having doors slammed in their faces. It's far easier to use words like angry, jealous and even ungrateful.

When I spoke in the press several years later about how it hurt to be looked over or rejected for roles or jobs that I knew I had both the talent and experience for, one black man sought to remind me that I was overstepping my boundaries.

'Urgh, you kind of women really fucking annoy me. You're sitting there wearing an expensive watch, you're a bestselling author, and yet you think this is about colourism? Don't you think you have enough? You're coming across as ungrateful. Maybe those people are just the better ones for the job.'

Without a second thought he was blocked from my social spaces, because as weathered as I was for this kind of behaviour from black men, I didn't want women who looked exactly like me to catch a stray from his self-hating gun. He was the same kind of man that would have attended a vigil if one of the Kardashians stubbed their toe – uninterested in their current or past accomplishments or wardrobes heaving with designer garments, he would simply have wanted to pet the head of a woman the world has told him is worthy of his tears, of his commiseration. I've learned through experience that words like 'gratitude' and 'lucky', and the mere idea of wanting too much, are usually only retained for the women who are at the bottom of the totem pole.

'Oh, not you, sweetie – you've got half a mule. And look at you. You're lucky to even have that. You're not desirable enough, not worthy enough to cry about the other half, least of all the forty acres you were promised. That promise wasn't yours, anyhow. So how dare you make a fuss about something that was never for you.'

This success, this happiness, this love, was never ever for you. So how dare you complain about not having it.

There are some women who look a lot like me who would join ranks with that man and agree, it's never for us.

This was highlighted to me by a very light-skinned friend who pointed out that because I seem to have done alright for myself, all things considered, others would try to pick holes in my experience every time I attempt to shed light on this issue, which has long been swept under the carpet. It appears that I have been able to slip through the net of a certain class, dodge the right hook of cultural and societal expectations and then long jump over the multitude of hurdles like misogynoir, sexism and racism, to arrive at the finish line with my entire being still intact. For those reasons alone there are dark-skinned women like me who are deeply turned off and triggered when I have the gall to say that things still aren't fair for me and, by implication, for us.

And I understand it. We have been conditioned to be grateful in the face of being disrespected and short-changed. I understand how it must feel, to see a reflection of yourself who is still demanding that her three bags full need topping up when those left behind are too exhausted, too hurt, too upset to even complain that they are only holding one. I understand how one of us sticking our head above the parapet and saying, 'You all are still not doing right by us' can bring about deep annoyance.

But it is exactly these unicorn-like victories and experiences which make me double down on colourism. By some luck of the draw, I am able to speak with more people than women like I have ever been told will listen to us. I've been able to pull up a chair at tables which usually make it clear that for dark-skinned black women, there isn't any space. I've been able to publish a book like this one. So being silent about this experience – be it because those who benefit from colourism want me to shut up, or because those who look more like me don't want me to rock the proverbial boat – is not an option. The more space I get, the louder this experience will become. Because dark-skinned black women should not have to suffer being an anomaly, the last choice or altogether erased. Sis, I said I understood, not that I would conform. And this attitude wasn't built in, it was definitely sold separately. Any wavering in my often flimsy convictions that I was in fact 'wonderfully made' really had to firm up once I was a parent. Especially when I found out I was going to be the mother to a little girl, a little black girl who would still not be free of the pain of colourism.

When Esmé was born, I watched her like a hawk. Of course, all mothers do. By the time she was born, there was nothing to do but go on Mumsnet and worry myself. Got to check she's breathing every ten seconds. Is she eating enough? Is that cry normal? But that wasn't the only thing I was keeping an eye on. I was also keen to see how her complexion would develop. I didn't want her to be as dark as me. To hear the painful disses in the playground. For South Asian hair shop owners to try and sell her some bleaching creams at the till. For her to constantly feel inferior alongside her lighter-skinned or mixed-race classmates.

If you're the mother to a black baby, you know good and well that their skin tone at birth isn't usually long-lasting. To conduct the 'true colour' test, one must look at the tips of the ears. I must have done that every day until she was about two years old. And I wasn't alone in this. I have dark-skinned friends who, whether they realise it or not, have an unmistakable joviality in their voice and lightness (pardon the pun) when their child has lighter skin than them and they get to share that. This is the space in which they would, if they could without judgement, express their relief at having a child who might not be so unfairly scrutinised due to their complexion. When I noticed this, I had to admit that me constantly watching Esme's own complexion was part of the problem. If she was the same complexion or darker than me, at least she had a mother who 'got it' and had in no way sought to change herself. I now had a living, breathing reason to be the best example of self-acceptance I could muster.

And right on time, she's beginning to notice some things herself.

'Yeah, but she's not brown like me, Mummy. I'm very brown.'

'So why do they call us black? Look! I'm not the same as this!' she sighed, holding a black crayon up against her face, trying to make a very valid point.

One of our favourite books to read together is *Sulwe* by Lupita Nyong'o. It smartly tells the story of colourism through the eyes of a very dark-skinned little girl who often wished she was as light-skinned as her parents and sister. When I first read it, I had to quickly turn away and wipe away a tear. It had taken thirty years for me to see myself in a storybook. Wow.

One evening as we finished the book, Esme said to me: 'You are darker than me, Mummy. You are like Sulwe.'

'Exactly,' I answered. 'And all you have to remember is that being a darker shade of brown is not a bad thing. It's a beautiful thing, like Sulwe.' I smiled, rubbing my finger along her cheek like my father used to do to me.

I think it's important that I admit that I didn't have the same worries about my son, RJ. Whilst I would be lying if I said that colourism doesn't affect dark-skinned black men, it would be equally untrue for me to ignore the differences. Most dark-skinned black men aren't demonised due to their skin tone – in fact, it's sensationally the opposite. They are usually hypersexualised. Tall, dark and handsome, they call it. Long used as the centre of white women's sexual fantasies, dark-skinned black men are usually able to sidestep the more painful encounters their dark-skinned sistas endure by playing up to the role of being an insatiable lover boy. Experience had taught me that it is most usually those men, dark-skinned black men, who would be the unkindest to those that look exactly like them. Of which I have too many experiences to count.

So, my worries for my son are different. I worry that without me noticing, he may become the kind of black man who will kiss me and carry my shopping but then tell a dark-skinned black woman she is the ugliest thing he has ever seen. I worry that he will take pictures with myself and his sisters but then feel ashamed to stand alongside women of the same hue who aren't his family. I worry that society will get him good and proper and he will fall for the fallacy that acquiring a light-skinned or mixed-race partner is akin to the golden ticket to Willy Wonka's chocolate factory. Will he choose a light-skinned partner not because he truly loves them, but because it's how the world will dictate that he has 'arrived'? I often wonder. But more about that in the next lesson.

Of course, there are those who, like the All Lives Matter crew, will say that this idea I have about colourism is merely that, an idea. Not a true, lived experience. A lot like the beneficiaries of racism, there will be lighter-skinned people reading this who will be terribly affronted. And, like their white counterparts, the easiest way to not have to listen nor understand the fact that they have privilege due to their skin tone is to shut the conversation down entirely. There will be cries of, 'Well, it's not all of us.' 'All of this talk is just dividing us further.' 'I didn't ask to be light-skinned – it's not easy for me either.' And a whole host of other pushbacks and reasons as to why they need not engage with this conversation, let alone think about how they could use some of that privilege to help their dark-skinned sistas fight against this unfair hierarchy, or at least speak with those who have more power than they do.

A great positive example of this was when Amandla Stenberg backed out of playing Shuri, the sister of King T'challa in *Black Panther*, so that Letitia Wright could go on to play the role. 'These are all dark-skinned actors playing Africans, and I feel like it would have just been off to see me as a biracial American with a Nigerian accent just pretending that I'm the same colour as everyone else in the movie,' Stenberg said. 'I recognize 100 per cent that there are spaces that I should not take up.' I think that move was bold and important. But it's not one I think many are going to choose to make.

The reality is – just like its bigger, broader, older cousin racism – combating colourism is going to take a very long time. Asking anyone to relinquish or check for privilege that, in one way or another, makes their lived experience more comfortable is going to be met with resistance on all sides. And unlike racism, colourism doesn't affect the entire black race, it only negatively affects a chosen few. Data and my lived experience prove that there is very little acceptance of the problem, let alone support within our own spaces. If fighting against racism takes black people holding hands, facing outwards and saying, 'It's them,' deconstructing colourism will take us linking arms, forming a circle, facing each other and saying, 'It's us.' And there are far too few people willing to do that. And that's why although I've personally never set foot on a slave plantation, I have sure as hell felt the division that was only ever devised by 'them' to force a wider wedge between 'us'.

And because I just don't see that happening during a time frame that will allow me to enjoy this sharing of power, this ease that I keep talking about, I have to work really hard to ensure that I keep myself topped up, that I keep my spirits high. That when I get in certain spaces or catch a certain blessing, I scoot over or share said blessing with other dark-skinned black women who are also feeling the pressure of a construct that keeps its foot on our necks.

Slowly, things are changing, and as ever we have the internet to thank for this. Now more than ever there is a plethora of dark-skinned black women utilising platforms like YouTube to share and discuss the content and experiences that speak directly to us. The democratisation that the internet provides is giving dark-skinned black women the stage and the micro-phone and of course, I am loving every minute of it. Naturally the cosmetic industry is following the internet's lead and we are having what is coined the 'Fenty Effect'. All of a sudden, big names in the beauty industry have begun to notice that dark-skinned black women exist! No longer are we having to put up with the darkest shade of foundation available still being six shades too light. Many thank Rihanna for this, as when she announced her make-up line 'Fenty Beauty', she made a point of starting with no less than forty shades of foundation, including some of the darkest shades I've seen to date.

Whilst she is by no means at the helm of the first beauty company to try and include the needs and desires of darker-skinned women in their offerings, her celebrity, combined with the current cultural zeitgeist – and most importantly, how well produced both the marketing and product actually are – made it very clear to other make-up brands that they needed to buck up their ideas and fast. But of course they would; they have finally realised that, by not including dark-skinned black women when it comes to formulating beauty products, they aren't getting our coin.

When it comes to traditional media, the changes are happening but at a far slower pace. Sure, we have the broad-casting powerhouse Clara Amfo, TV genius Michaela Coel, actress Susan Wokoma and influencer and businesswoman Patricia Bright, but considering how long it's taken me to think about how many dark-skinned black women are actu-ally able to succeed in their respective spaces is a mark of just how dire things are. And don't get it twisted – just because I haven't listed an entire page of dark-skinned black women doesn't mean there aren't hundreds of thousands doing great work; the problem is that we aren't given enough room to shine. It's just not good enough.

To this day, I'm glad I had the courage to say that col-ourism still affects me. Whilst love, a family unit and a career I'm passionate about are now the first things I think of in the morning, instead of how I can defend myself against terms like 'blick', doesn't mean that I've been able to escape this all-consuming idea that because of the tone of my skin, I'm not beautiful or worthy. The times between the incidents and reminders are becoming wider but that doesn't mean they are disappearing entirely.

What I am finding is that I am ending up in spaces where I have more control, and I am able to be the voice at a table that can point out where colourism is at play. I'm now able to bend the ear of people who can give the gatekeepers a nudge.

And listen, irrespective of being a dark-skinned black women, I'm coming for my forty acres and the other half of my mule. And I won't stop until I get it.

What I wish I'd known:

- Learning not to be affected by colourism is impossible. But building up your confidence so that you can take the inevitable rejections that will arise because you are dark-skinned is something you can and should work on, daily.
- More often than not, many of the people who teased or rejected you because of your skin tone have self-hate issues you can't begin to imagine. Your very image is a reflection of a part of themselves they've been trained to dislike. It's hard to understand right now, but the attacks aren't personal to you; the slurs are actually about them.
- You have a right to call out colourism. Point, blank, period.
- You are beautiful. One day your skin tone will be seen as an asset not as a liability.

Lesson 8

JUNGLE FEVER - ON MEN

Now, don't judge me, but I have worn acrylic nails for the last fifteen years. Aside from when I went travelling in India, when I had two babies and when I stayed at home during the lock-downs, I can hardly remember a time that I have looked down and not seen my beloved long artificial talons shining back at me. One of the things I love most is the experience of going to nail salons. There is something undeniably intersectional about them. One of my regular spots is run by a petite Asian woman who at times I feel knows more about my life than I do. And it's not my life alone she's able to retain an encyclopaedic level of information about – she knows the isms and schisms of every single one of her regulars, these women of all races, shapes and sizes, who, whilst picking a particular shade of pink nail varnish and having their cuticles pushed back, find themselves using that time as a miniature therapy session.

There are two types of people who enter the nail salon. The first are those who want to entertain and be entertained in equal measure. Then there are those who have come for a bit of peace and quiet. The latter are polite, but they will speak only if spoken to. I am sure of this because I am firmly in that camp.

Aside from giving out the odd instruction after the obligatory pleasantries and greetings, I would much rather be entertained by strangers. I find listening to other people fascinating. Plus, there isn't anything which clears my head like having to doing nothing but swap my hands under a UV light. The last time I went to the nail salon, I was surprised to find it was only me in there. Just as I started to zone out, a lady came in with a voice that immediately made me know that we were in for a treat. And she did not disappoint. Before a nail tech even had the chance to remove the nail varnish she had come in with, I had learned that her almost three-year-old had a habit of trying to eat his own excrement, she had put back on the stone in weight she had lost before the first national lockdown and, most importantly, that her boyfriend of nine years had finally (her word – not mine) proposed to her.

'Ooh, what colour should I have?' she squealed, asking no one in particular. 'It needs to be something that brings out this bit of bling!' she exclaimed, thrusting her left hand into the air and wriggling her fingers about.

She carried on, not caring if anyone was listening. 'We won't be able to get married until 2023! And can you believe that a month before he proposed to me, my sister's fella proposed! It was gonna be handbags at dawn! And my sister was helping him plan his proposal to me! I do hope she doesn't feel like I've stolen her thunder. But it wouldn't be the first time!' She laughed.

On and on she went about the upcoming marriage. And then finally, after about an hour, the owner of the nail shop asked her how her business was going. It turned out that she ran a highly successful hair salon on the other side of town. Her reaction to the question astounded me: she just shrugged her shoulders, and suddenly looked utterly bored and disinterested.

'Oh, really well, thanks. We've been so busy, and I've almost finalised the contract on getting a new space.' Her voice was nowhere as buoyant with excitement as it had been just before.

I sighed. I was clearly eavesdropping on yet another case of 'catching a man', and that being the most exciting thing that could ever happen to a woman. I firmly jabbed my Air-Pods deep into my ears and put them on noise-cancellation mode.

Growing up, I realised early on that women seemed to be obsessed with what men thought of them. The popular reading material at the time was books such as *Men Are from Mars, Women Are from Venus* and *He's Just Not That Into You*. Oh, and it wasn't just the books; the most popping movies all seemed to be centred on a woman getting her heart broken or getting over a heartbreak. Even the more age-appropriate shows – mostly American sitcoms like *Moesha, Sister, Sister* and my favourite movie/sitcom of all time, *Clueless* – seemed to be comfortable in regurgitating storylines that always showed girls wanting to get a guy to notice them. So, by the time I was old enough to even think about having a boyfriend, I was already conditioned to expect that it was my duty to catch their eye and then try my hardest to keep their vision fixed on me. But what most of this educational material didn't take into consideration was that I looked like . . . well . . . me. The fact was, I was never in their line of sight. I guess you could say that I had a twisted head start when it came to failed relationships with men.

I remember a light-skinned friend of mine once said her older brother had some friends we should link. Back then, when I was at secondary school, that was slang for 'meeting up with people' but in this moment it actually meant 'hook up with some boys to see if you're girlfriend material, so wear lip gloss, stick your B-cup tits out and appear just on the right side of aloof'. This was when I was desperately trying to break out of my studious, geeky shell; I had learned to slick my edges to within an inch of their lives. My senses were on constant high alert so that if a group of boys passed us, I could whip my thick-lensed glasses off at a moment's notice and trick even God Himself into believing that I had 20/20 vision. I had even taken to nabbing one of my mother's cigarettes when she wasn't looking so I could put one behind my ear, like the others did. Yeah, that was me: a proper bad gyal.

So, I was ready. I was sure that today would be my day.

After school, the boys came to meet us at the gates. I so desperately wanted to be approved of that I cannot remark on what any of them looked like – plus, of course I didn't have my glasses on. But I do remember the sniggering and pointing when my friend was like, 'This is Candice, isn't she beautiful?' whilst gently pushing me towards the boys.

'She's OK, I guess,' the ringleader said, shrugging. 'But you know how I feel about darkies.' His eyes fell briefly on me as if my mere physicality proved his point. 'I'd like to know *her* better,' he went on, gesturing towards Jaz, a quiet and equally as short-sighted Bengali girl in our friendship group. After a few more minutes of clearly not being wanted, I made some unheard excuses, turned on my heel and cried so much on the way home that I shouldn't have bothered to put my glasses back on.

For me, I was always faced with the conundrum that the love and affection the two primary black men in my life – my father and my grandfather – showered on me since I was a baby was not going to be how all black men felt about me. I had to understand that outside was a different story. If I was to ever feel the love that existed outside of those male bonds, then I was going to either have to lower my standards or change my approach entirely. I had spent most of my childhood being the 'ugly friend', so I was very prepared to face more romantic rejection than my peers, but that didn't mean that the pinch that follows this kind of disregard hurts any less.

Also, I had reached an age where the conversations surrounding having a boyfriend were becoming more of a thing that everyone wanted to be a part of.

When I was younger, I would cover the sting that comes with a boy saying he would 'rather be chased by a dog with rabies' than have me involved in a game of kiss chase with a fake but firm retort that no one wanted to play with boys anyhow. But now I was getting older, it was getting harder to keep that façade going. Every girl wanted to be liked by someone – at least, that was how it seemed.

And it's how it still seems now.

I am deeply concerned by how becoming someone's wife is still being upheld as the ultimate prize. Recently I came across a person's social media profile. In the space for the biography – which, at the most egotistical point in the spectrum, is used to reel off achievements and awards, and at its most basic, usually states the person's name, job title or even their hobby – it simply said 'Wife'. OK, I'm lying, there was also a ring emoji. But that was it. Just 'Wife'. I slowly tilted my phone back and forth as if it were a hologram about to reveal something else, but of course nothing else appeared. Long after I had found another way to fill my time, I could not help but wonder who this woman was. What was her name? What did she enjoy doing? Was she a receptionist? A dancer? A neurosurgeon? And why on earth did it bother me so much that the only thing she wanted to share was the fact she was married.

I know that as a feminist, I should be able to let it go, as that was her choice. But I couldn't help it. Even though I have a significant other with two children and a dog, this is not the information that I like to lead with. From awkward round-table discussions to the filler conversations you have to have before you are seated at an evening event, I never include my marital status in my introductory banter. Name? Of course. Recent achievements? My ego would die if I didn't go there. But married or single? I just don't think it's that important.

It's galling to think we are in a time where women can do many things, including be vice president in the highest office in the land, and yet some of us still feel silently judged by society based on our relationship status. Although I understand the pressures, I personally feel like announcing the fact that someone wanted to make you their wife is . . . boring. Not only that, it implies that anything else you have achieved is simply a stepping-stone to that point. Now, more than ever, I would love to see all talk of marriage, babies and relationships to be add-ons, the appendix, something that is separate to one's core identity rather than a definition of one's worthiness as a woman.

Since the beginning of my time, I have had front row seats to watching black women sacrifice every molecule of themselves to bag a man. I have also watched too many black women allow their spirits to curl up and die because being in an unhappy relationship seemed better than being in no relationship at all. Being with a man who only came to check you on a Thursday and Friday with the audacity to still be smelling like the women he had cheated on you with on Monday to Wednesday was better than spending the entire week alone.

Now, as you already know, I am no self-love saint. I struggle at the best of times with negative thoughts, skewed body image and low self-confidence. Since as far back as I can remember, men who look like me have made it clear that I am their last choice, because of my blackness – and that doesn't seem to have changed. I was jolted into real-ising just how commonplace this idea still is by a tweet I recently saw by a black man, in which he outlined his order of preferences:

WHITE GIRLS

MIXED GIRLS

LATINA GIRLS

ASIAN GIRLS

A CORPSE

BLACK GIRLS

You see, I know that being a black woman makes me extra sensitive to the things we supposedly need to do or be before being considered valuable enough to take off the shelf. In most instances I have seen this process have less than desirable outcomes.

Reading that man's list of preferences again brought back the earlier rejections I had experienced – being told that I was never 'top tier', on top of the hurt inflicted by the hundreds, if not thousands, of social media videos that illustrate just how unappealing it is to even consider being in a relationship with a dark-skinned black woman – that had always been lingering just beneath the surface. Now they began to haunt me again.

'You know, usually I would never, never be with a dark-skinned girl. You're just not my type,' one boyfriend said with a sigh as he stroked my nose. 'But you're kind of cute, so you can stay a while.'

He laughed, and I laughed too, because what else do you do when your self-esteem is somewhere below the heap of clothes that were ripped off and thrown to the floor just before you had sex? Exactly. It was an extremely vulnerable moment, and particularly crushing as he was older than me and I looked up to him. For some reason, being with an older guy was what you did. When my friends and I were sixteen and seventeen, the standard was that your boyfriend had to be in his early to mid-twenties. Now, although no one could get arrested for that, I admit that retrospectively something about it doesn't feel right.

I don't care how many cigarettes you've smoked, tampons you've used, or even if you can drive. Speaking from experience, the only thing a high percentage of men in their forties could ever want from a woman who has just said goodbye to her teenage years is the chance to not only fuck her but also fuck her over. No amount of make-up could conceal how little I thought of myself, and older men seemed to be able to read me and my insecurities like a book, and then use them to manipulate me. Of course, there are some relationships with Grand Canyon-sized age gaps that seem to go the distance, but the vast majority of them rely on a woman that young being a plaything.

After routinely being mocked, rejected, or just simply overlooked by boys in my community, it became clear that me holding out for 'black love' was a waste of my time. So, when I was in my twenties, I dated many white guys who were much older than me. One in particular never wanted to hold hands in public. And he only ever introduced me as his 'very dear' friend. His mates were polite enough, but one woman I met got right to the heart of the matter. One night we ended up at a party where everyone was already completely off their faces, so what tumbled out of her mouth was perhaps not surprisingly unfiltered.

'She's very pretty,' she cooed, talking about me as if I had left the room, when in fact I was standing right in front of her. 'But I've seen them all come and go. They are always so young. And you tell me you don't have a thing for black girls? Come on! Also, how long until she gets pissed off with you for stringing her along? Always a young trophy, never a wife.'

She then offered me something to drink.

I hastily snatched the tumbler from her and drank what was inside in one go, so I did not immediately have to process what had just happened. In a quick burst of vocalised thoughts, she had helped me identify several red flags. Flags that had always caught my attention, but I had become routinely blind to. The reality was, I did not want to be alone forever. So, if older white dudes were going to bless me with some much-needed attention, however qualified, that I could dress up as love, then I would have to get on with it. To say that white men were my preference didn't come naturally to me, but what else was there to do? And so, the period of my life which can be summed up as 'jungle fever' – defined by the Urban Dictionary as a person's preference for an interracial sexual or romantic relationship – began.

Such is the law of attraction that the minute I made that decision, my aura must have begun to radiate an 'I only date white boys' vibe, because all of a sudden white men became very receptive to my sexual energy. I say sexual because, now I have hindsight on my side, I don't think I've ever, *ever* been with a white man who wasn't fulfilling his own jungle fever fetish on his end. But back then, in that moment, you couldn't tell me shit. This was love.

Do you know how light my heart felt when a man finally allowed the heaviness of his palm to envelop my own, in public? Sis, it was like a dream come true. Words cannot describe how it feels to be wanted, even if your subconscious suspects that it perhaps has more to do with *what* you are rather than *who* you are. I have come to find out that there is so very much a lonely heart will overlook. But whilst I was enjoying this newfound attention, there were others who weren't so keen on the idea of me dating outside of my race.

'Now, Queen, why would you disrespect your own like

that?' one black man questioned as I strolled down the street, hand in hand with an alabaster-toned boyfriend.

I kissed my teeth.

'Aww, don't be like that, Empress, you know you want to be with a king like me!' he called after us.

I felt the boyfriend's grip on my hand become decidedly looser.

I so desperately wanted to turn around and ask the black man a few things:

If I'm such a queen, why is it that you black men refuse to see my crown until a man of another race wants to help straighten it for me?

Why is it that you all are so fast to marry anyone as long as they don't look like your mama?

And for the few of you who do decide to settle down with black women, why is it most of you are intent on ruining your queen's self-esteem and your own home by cheating with women we are then forced to feel we are competing with?

But I was enjoying having my hand held, the sun was blazing and the yellow summer dress I was wearing really accentuated my melanin, so I decided to keep on stepping. It seemed I was invisible to black men until the spotlight put upon me by a white man made me visible.

Not only have cackle-filled conversations with my dark-skinned black sisters solidified and supported all my thoughts and experiences, but we have data to back us up too. Research (which was later deleted) from dating site OkCupid shows that in 2014, black women were considered the least desirable by all races of men; so, for anyone wondering: nope, it is not just in our heads. Now, even if you constantly work on your confidence and try to ignore society's commitment to undermine and overlook the beauty of black women who aren't considered exotic (caramel skin, green eyes, and hair with looser curls instead of kinks), what I can't look past is all that is fed to us in the media. When was the last time you saw a man who is black with an equally black woman? And Bode and I don't count! It's OK, I'll wait; I might even go and make a flat white. Because the truth is, they are very few and far between.

I remember watching the BRIT Awards a few years ago and commenting on my Instagram account that there didn't seem to be many darker-skinned black women up for awards, even though the UK music scene is awash with musical talent coming from these women. Instantly, DMs came flooding in. My black sistas were like 'amen', and white women admitted they had never noticed, but now that I had pointed this out, it was all they could think about. And how could I blame the latter for not noticing? Especially when there is a large number of black men who, once they have successfully transcended the upper echelons of their workplace or found their public profile has exploded, seem to find a significant other who is anything but black. It is not for me to judge what is going on inside their relationships, but I do often wonder if they ever stop to think about why their preference seems to be everything they are not.

Whilst many black men seem to date and marry outside of their race due to their preference, I have found that many black women do so out of necessity. I'll say it again: most black women I know, myself included, would never say that white men were their preference, because it usually isn't so. Most of us just got tired of waiting for a black man, only for him to show us ridicule and heartache.

Now, I think it's important to encourage women to go where the love is. So, if that means widening your dating net to experience being with people who aren't the same race as you, I would ask you to do that without hesitation. I've spoken with women who wanted children and watched their biological window slam shut because they were waiting for one type of man who was clearly running on Black People Time. Now they are in their fourth decade, trying to not only grapple with dating apps, but also the realisation that they were waiting to bat for men who weren't even going to show up to the field. But, speaking from experience, it would be poor form of me not to issue a warning. As a black woman I have found that dipping my toe into the interracial sea has not been without its choppy waters.

There was one guy – for the sake of not wanting to be sued, let us call him Adam. We dated for a while – and just to be clear, we actually went out, in public, to bars and concerts and stuff. Before that, I thought dating was someone taking you to the movies once, never introducing you to his friends, and only ever returning your call once the sun had set and he was horny. Like most women, I was aware (read that as 'hoping') that the moment I would meet his family was just around the corner. But instead, it was always us meeting for drinks or dinner. At a push he would take me along to a friend's birthday party. Whilst he did not introduce me as a friend, he never used the term girlfriend, either. By the time we had been going steady for nine months, I had lost all patience. One late evening after one too many cocktails, as we were walking through a children's park play area, it all came tumbling out of me. After I tongue-lashed him for a firm twenty minutes, he looked at me, surprised.

'Candice, do you know where I'm from?' he asked with a tone that implied the question was rhetorical. 'I'm from a place where people would still refer to you as coloured. The youngest members of my family have never even met a black person. It all makes sense in this multicultural metropolis, but outside of this space, I just do not see a future for us. I admire the fact you see the world in colour – I think it is what I like most about you. But I see the world in black and white. And I just do not think this will work long-term,' he admitted, looking down at the grass.

Even writing about this brings tears to my eyes.

As humiliated and hurt as I was, I knew better than to beg. After throwing some expletives his way, I turned on my heel and left both him and the idea of us ever being together behind. I couldn't believe I had been so stupid, so naive. So depleted of love and validation was I, I hadn't recognised that to him, I was simply fulfilling a fantasy (remember what I said about white men and their fetish). It was like he'd gone on a porn website, selected 'ebony', jerked off and then deleted his browser history so no one would know about his dirty little secret.

Unfortunately, neither one of us was banking on a future where the difficulties of making both our fantasies a reality would be so significant. And in some respects, I don't think either of us could begin to comprehend the Pandora's box we had just opened. Even though I never went back on my word, I dated many more Adams. White men who seemed to tick every box, until it came to taking the relationship to the next level, which, for one reason or another, they could never do. I seemed to be caught in no man's land (pardon the pun). Rejected by the men who looked the most like me and not quite loved by those who didn't. Perpetually unloveable.

That's tough to describe and talk about. Really, the seeds

of this were planted years before I could truly recognise the impact that they were having. As I mentioned before, it was never seeing women who look like you as main characters in romcoms or dramas. It was only ever seeing one on the cover of a magazine if there had been an outcry about the lack of diversity, and for a moment everyone felt they had to prove their allyship. It was watching the men in your community leave their black girlfriends to make a white woman their wife. Sometimes it was black men leaving their black wives for their white mistresses, whilst their black daughters looked on, unaware of how much that would go on to affect their psyches. Of course, I am often told – almost exclusively by those who are not black – that I am overthinking it. Or that I just need to accept that everyone has a preference. Or that black women could keep black men if they were less argumentative, more docile, more 'put up and shut up'.

But it does make you think, right? There was even an instance when I spoke about how I was working hard to ensure that my own son isn't conditioned to believe that black women like his mother are unloveable and ugly. I expressed how I hoped that he would see the value in black women and in the idea of black love. A white woman reached out to tell me how my thoughts had worried her, as her husband was black and he had always made a point of saying how he did not find black women attractive. My words had now made her wonder if, to him, she was simply a question of aesthetic preference. She wondered if by marrying her, he had assumed he had married up and out of his blackness.

I was never going to answer her, but before I could, she erased her message and apologised for overstepping. She understood these were questions for him. Indeed, they were.

None of these questions are for black women.

Because when it comes to protecting and uplifting black men, we are on the frontline. To then be forced to answer questions as to why that is not reciprocated is a step too far.

As for me, after realising that I could perhaps be stuck in this uncomfortable in-between forever, I resigned myself to appearing to be anti-love. It seemed that you could either be played or do the playing. I would have to get used to doing the latter, because being the former was far too much for my heart to bear.

As chaotic and dangerous as some of my life choices seemed, when it came to my devoid-of-love love life, it looked like I was having fun. And I won't lie to you, some parts were incredibly fun. Those moments made up for the pang of jealousy I would feel when I got another Facebook notification telling me that another schoolmate had just got married. They almost blotted out my deep desire to be loved altogether. Almost. And it is because of that that I can see through most young women's anti-love rhetoric.

I understand why it's there, and I respect its importance. God knows how many more heartbreaks that my 'love is for the weak!' attitude saved me from. But I also now know how lucky I was that my desire to have this genuine, loving transaction with someone was not erased entirely. Because now I am here. And I would want anyone to end up here, should they truly desire it too.

And where is here exactly?

In love with a black man.

Sis, I know.

Sometimes I can't believe it either. And nor can those I grew up with. If I happen to be out and bump into an old friend, I have to stifle laughter at their obvious confusion when I introduce my husband.

'Girl, I know I ain't seen you in a hot minute, but I cannot believe you are with a black man! Miracles really do happen!' one of them said, chuckling, as we caught up after years of having drifted apart.

I couldn't even correct her; it felt like a miracle indeed. But not like that. That whole, 'Oh, aren't you lucky to have a man' – we don't do that here. Because that is often the conclusion people end up with. If you have ever identified as someone who for whatever reason has been deemed unloveable, the last choice or eternally single, and gone on to find a happy relationship, many want to remind you how lucky you are to have found someone who does find you attractive enough to stick around. Oh, lucky me!

No. The true miracle was that I had let my guard down long enough to be loved.

And you know, props to Bode, I did not make it easy for him. In many ways, he has had to pay for the times when an ex didn't want to introduce me as a girlfriend or when Adam dumped me in that park. He has had to prove to me time and time again that his love for me is genuine. And along with learning how to love me, he has had to be stable enough to stand by me as I've fallen in and out of love with myself whilst we both managed the expectations of society, which are more often than not never far away.

It is not lost on me how many women are enraged by the fact that I am with a man who publicly loves me so deeply. I am always on standby to help others unpick this initial knee-jerk reaction of disbelief to the fact that he is married to a dark-skinned black woman – me – who, like Cardi B raps, doesn't do the cooking or the cleaning. It's usually not personal to me, but often down to a messy cocktail of three shots of misogynoir, a measure of patriarchy and a sprinkling of low self-esteem. I, more than anyone, truly understand how affronting it is to see a woman – whom the world has repeatedly placed at the bottom of the pile – suddenly being held up high. I get that it can bring out feelings in others who are perceived as prettier, perkier, and better packaged as truly 'wifey' material – feelings which can range from discomfort and jealousy to outright anger, whether they admit it to themselves or not.

Few things make me feel sadder than to watch these women contort themselves into becoming everything they have been tricked into thinking the opposite sex will find attractive, only to end up in relationships which over time lose their shine. Not only will they have settled for less than they deserve, but they have also perhaps offered up a version of themselves which is not a reflection of their most authentic selves at all.

But all this waffling is not to say that I know it all or that my understanding of men and relationships is the be-all and end-all. However, I will say that just like condoms and cars, it really is not one size fits all. When we step away from the archaic societal expectations of heterosexual long-term relationships, it's amazing to see how many versions are on offer, if we're able to put the judgements of others on mute.

These thoughts didn't become crystal clear to me until a recent therapy session during which we discussed my pending nuptials.

'Well, you don't seem excited,' my therapist observed, somewhat coyly. 'I'm just trying to figure out why that is?' She smiled, cocking her head to one side in the way that she does that lets me know she has found her sweet spot.

We were already twenty-five minutes into a fifty-minute session, so I was fired up and ready to go.

'There are just more exciting things in life, you know?'

She didn't say anything. Instead, she let a silence hang, during which I remembered she wasn't one to fill in the blanks.

'A wedding day, a marriage, neither of those things define how much I love him. If it were solely about love, why couldn't we just remain . . . in love?' I sighed. 'For me, this is business. There are assets and a legacy to protect. I trust him to be my next of kin and in the unfortunate event of my premature death, I don't want anyone else thinking they have more of a say about how my affairs are conducted than the man I've shared a bed with for almost a decade. No one knows me like he does. But to marry solely for love? I think that is a bit much. And I'm a Pisces. So that's saying something.'

Even she couldn't stifle her giggles.

And you know, I mean what I said. This is not to say that I look down upon those couples whose sole reason for getting married is because they love each other. That is undisputedly one of the most romantic things ever. The thing is, I think because of my experience of trying to be loved and being rejected, that gold no longer glittered. I could see almost everyone around me throw themselves headfirst into marriages with more concern for how to make their wedding day go viral than how they might perhaps truly feel about lifetime monogamy, including watching their husband chewing with their mouth open. Bode and I were together for a long while, so I was gifted more time to think about what I didn't want and what made sense to me. And for love to be the only factor in two becoming one, well, that felt a little batshit crazy to me.

Bode and I had taken the Israelites' journey, the long way around. We had faced things some couples don't come up against until they are four decades deep into their union. And because our relationship didn't follow a conventional template, and because a black man committing long-term to a black woman is still a rarity, we have often found our relationship being held in high regard, which is deeply uncomfortable for us both.

I understand I have to take some responsibility here. Whilst I wanted to show on my social media that black nuclear families, who sit down and eat dinner together, do exist, it was never ever my plan to be an advocate for #BlackLove. And to be honest, I still am not. After my experiences with men of a variety of races, I think it would be insincere of me to preach that this should be the first or only kind of love black women specifically should be looking for. The reality is that black women have got to align themselves with the idea that we are entitled to go where the love is, whatever the colour. Even if that makes others uncomfortable. The deep truth is that unfortunately the most commonplace trends and behaviours of our male counterparts still suggest that the love and support we require is still not available to us. So, what are we to do?

I often joke that if Bode kicks the bucket before me, no one would be more shocked than me if I find the strength to move on. I already know that the likelihood of me being loved by another black man in the same way is highly unlikely. And whilst I've already said that it wasn't down to luck, I will admit that I have been spoilt by the way that he loves me, and I doubt a man of any other race would be able to bestow me with what he has. Even though I usually avoid any kind of gushiness, what has happened here truly feels as though it is the kind of magic you may only get to be the receiver of once in a lifetime.

As I mentioned, now I am the mother of a black son, I do often find myself to be heavily preoccupied with how he will think and talk about black women. I do worry a lot because most, if not all, the black boys and men who write tweets like the one I quoted earlier in this essay have mothers who look like them, mothers who look like me. And to be clear, it's not the stating of a preference I have a problem with, it's the absolute rubbishing of black women in the process that I won't stand for. I think it is lackadaisical to suggest that it's only the infrastructure of white supremacy, the white gaze and all forms of media pushing a rhetoric of 'white is right' to blame. I believe so much of this work begins at home.

A conversation with a male friend helped highlight my fears:

'I remember when my wife came round for dinner when she was still my girlfriend. After she left, a few of my uncles were like, you know you can do better than a black woman, right? Even my mum suggested that I really think about moving forward without her as there were clearly prettier girls who were interested in me. And I knew by that she meant white. And my mum is a black woman.'

Whilst a lot of people would be shocked to hear this, this revelation didn't stun me at all. I've heard countless stories from the lips of black men which suggest that the first woman to ever make them question the worthiness of their love and affection for black women were their own mothers. Which is why I do genuinely worry about what I will consciously or subconsciously be teaching my son when it comes to upholding and respecting black women, not just in private but, most importantly, for all to see. Will he protect and uphold black women? Will he love one? Who knows? Only time will tell if I've been able to prevent him from becoming the kind of young man who so often made me question my own self-worth.

Time has taught me that relationships take constant

work. At certain times Bode and I have each had to spend time being the breadwinner, not just financially but emotionally too. There are some days Bode is bringing more to the table and there are some days I am bringing the gold home. This relationship is always teaching me something new and I'm still learning about how so much of it is about give and take. What is interesting to analyse now is how relationships are being sold, especially to heterosexual women, as something that shouldn't require very much work from them at all.

'Find a man making no less than seven figures a year!'

Or:

'You shouldn't have to bring anything more to the table because being yourself is enough.'

I hate to be that person to crush your dream, but it is just not true. Whilst I would have agreed with that rhetoric ten years ago, almost a decade down the line, I have to say that it doesn't really work out that way. Personally, I have found it best to grow with someone. Whenever I found the constant necessary communication of a relationship too much, my common retort to Bode was, 'I was who I was when you got here.'

I giggle now because he was who he was, too. But I was still so closed off to the idea of being in love with this man that I was not able to leave space for the fact that he was who he was and still is. Luckily, I became more flexible and he extended his patience and, as the years have gone on, we have become who we are together. One of the best things about that is the practice in building a legacy together. Yes, I admit there would have definitely been fewer financial stresses if I had been firm about marrying a man who was already a millionaire. But, listen, having dated a few of those, I was already aware of how men who are established in various ways will keep you around because you tickle their fancy, not because they respect you. Having to weather storms with someone allows both of you to shine and show your respective strengths, and that for me is where true respect is formed. And that respect is the greatest foundation for love. Because it won't always be sunshine and rainbows.

The year in which I write this has been a true example of how our deepest, most loving relationships aren't always safe from outside influences. Nothing will make you question the love you have for someone more than having to be with them twenty-four hours a day, with only one hour's grace period for three months or more. Being locked down with one another has forced us to confront the things that busy work and life schedules were the perfect hiding place for. Our relationship cannot be sustained by the momentary excitement of sex. Nor can it be held together by solely being partners in raising children. The monotony of having to face not only ourselves but also our two small children, day after day, has almost created an ocean between us. There have been times when we have been close to calling this relationship the Rollercoaster. And, as ever, the worst part of it is, it is usually when our individual selves are lost at sea.

I used to cringe when I would hear things such as: 'The most important relationship you can have is the one you have with yourself.'

I thought such things were plasters, words usually spoken by women who had just been shot out of a heartbreak cannon. I assumed they said these things as mere comforters amid the admin, the dissolving of assets and the reconfigurations of children's lives. Now it is with embarrassment I admit how important that truth is.

When I was racking up solo life experiences, fucking up, job- and bed-hopping, so consumed with what life had to offer, I didn't have the headspace to think about how beneficial a loving relationship with a man could be. Would such thinking perhaps have saved me from the more cruel or harsh experiences which seemed to be reserved for women that look like me? No. There is no excuse for the rambunctious and repetitive displays of disrespect and put-downs that typically come from our own. There are no words to take the sting off the after-effects. But perhaps I would have spent less time trying to be anything but me. Perhaps I would have opened myself up to a version of the kind of love I am now experiencing far sooner. Who knows, eh? Who knows?

What I wish I'd known:

- Black women specifically should not feel indebted to the idea of a relationship that is so often withheld from them. Confidently go where the love is.
- A marital status is no substitute for a personality trait.
- The love you receive from another cannot match the love you have for yourself.
- Like all relationships, interracial ones take work. And it is never too late to check if you are being fetishised or used as a preference to dissolve self-hatred.

Lesson 9

NINE NIGHTS AND FOREVER MORE – ON DEATH

One of the most common questions I am ever asked is, 'How do you stay motivated?' I live such a full life that I often do not realise how intense it can come across to those who on occasion peek into it. The crack is that I am very, very aware of how limited my time on this earth could be. Even if I lived long enough to call myself a centenarian, that really is no time at all. The thing that keeps me going, even when I am exhausted and feel there is nothing left to give, is the idea of death.

I think about death and dying a lot, usually multiple times a day.

Those closest to me would perhaps say that I am death-obsessed and I would be inclined to agree. Where most women my age perhaps spend hours watching YouTube videos that show current hauls and hacks, my viewing pleasures are of a different kind. Most of my evenings are spent researching women making waves in the death department. From embalmers to undertakers, I am fascinated with all things morbid. Even as a child, when walking past a funeral home, I would tug gently on my carer's arm, forcing them to slow down so I could really take in the beauty of all the headstones, urns and caskets in the window.

One of my favourite pastimes, which was curling up in my grandfather's lap and watching what was then called the World Wrestling Federation, also came with a side order of the unknown. I had a favourite wrestler called The Undertaker. Watching this almost seven-foot figure approach the ring, usually with his theatrical assistant Paul Bearer, would thrill me. On big fight nights, he would push a casket to the ring so that he could put his opponent right in it once he had destroyed him. I was both afraid and hypnotised.

Growing up, I could not understand why no one else was as consumed with death as I was. As young as I was, I understood it was a portal to another world, one which very few seemed to want to discuss. What I had yet to learn was that this is usually because death must also come with grief. They are rarely separate entities. As with all things, time would teach me that lesson.

I described finding out about my father's death in

Lesson 4. But what I didn't include was the aftermath, the full-on emotional toll of it all.

Let's fast forward to the early hours of the following morning, I found myself pulling my single black suitcase down the five flights of stairs to wait for my taxi outside. I remember being ridiculously early for it – I had half an hour to spare – but I needed to be out in the fresh air, with only the stars to keep me company. Although we were apparently in the middle of a harsh Naples winter, a nearby sign at a pharmacist's which rotated between telling the time and the weather let me know that even at this hour the temperature was in its early teens. Still, I had decided to wear my coat all the way home, so frozen I was inside. Pulling the vast hood of the coat up and over my head, I let the tears roll once more. I had only been able to pause them intermittently and it exhausted me even to try.

I also sporadically dialled Dad's mobile. Although I had spoken to various people who had explained that his death was due to extremely severe symptoms of the flu, I still could not quite believe it. I had only spoken with him a few days prior. Admittedly he had said he seemed to be bunged up with a cold, but to be on his deathbed so quickly wasn't making sense to me. As much as my body seemed to want to submit to the facts which would lead to the grieving process, it seemed my mind wouldn't allow me to do so until I had seen it, or rather him, for myself.

A week later, having barely slept, the time had come.

My maternal grandfather, the man I had perhaps regarded as my first father, had offered to escort me to the chapel of rest. As we approached the funeral home, I began to shake uncontrollably. He held me firmly by the shoulders.

'Listen, Boobie,' he began. 'This is perhaps the most adult thing you will ever do. And it is terrible, really. Your dad has died so young. But you must see this through.'

He reached into the inside pocket of his trusty mustard-and-pea-coloured coat.

He pressed a cold, silver flask into my palm.

'Here. Dutch courage.' He winked, gesturing for me to knock it back.

Usually, I would have pulled a face. But over the last week I had drunk more than a teenager at freshers' week. Even on the flight home, I had ripped open the bag containing some Jack Daniel's I had spent the last of my wages on in duty-free. The air hostess looked like she was going to tell me it was not allowed, but then she locked eyes with me, and I don't know if she registered my stare as anger or sadness, but either way, she offered up a shy smile and left me to it.

We were led into the funeral home by a man who didn't even try to hide the fact that he was very busy.

'Mi sarry fi yuh loss,' he mumbled quickly before trotting past the coffin and out a door at the other side of the room.

I held my breath. From where I stood, I could clearly see a cheap-looking wooden coffin with a figure in a suit lying in it. As I crept forward, I decided to drink in the decor to distract me from having to face the obvious. The entire room was painted baby blue. As my eyes looked upwards – anywhere but my father's body – I saw white shapes, which I can only assume were supposed to resemble clouds. As I tilted my head back further still, I saw they were actually cumulus-shaped cherubs linking arms to form an imperfect garland, which sat directly above where the coffin was positioned. A few of the cherubs were clasping trumpets, some were holding scrolls. All of them were white and smiling.

I was in hell.

'Oh, Rich. Oh, Rich. I'm sorry, kid.' Stood directly over the coffin, my grandfather cried as he stroked the face of the body I had still not looked at.

I inched closer, forcing my eyes to confront this reality. I began at the end. How odd: he was not wearing his shoes. Instead, they were placed awkwardly at the sides of his sock-covered feet, which were in first position, like a ballerina.

As I slowly took in the rest of the body, I noticed every imperfection in the stitching of the off-black suit he had been draped in. When I landed on the white gloved hands, I took a sharp breath. They were folded on top of each other as if he was patiently waiting for a child to explain why they had been caught sneaking cookies before dinner. I felt an urge to grab them and sharply pull them out of that pose. Soon my eyes were upon the collar of his white shirt. I noticed a stray hair which had made its way from his head onto the material. Later, I would learn that hair falls away from a dead body, as the functions that would usually keep it in place have since ceased their duties. It feels terribly obvious once you think about it.

Up to that point, I hadn't really been able to relate the dead body to my father. It could have been anyone lying there. But the chin was a dead giveaway. My father had a remarkably deep dimple under his mouth. Even though his skin was now ashen and cold, there it was, like a serial number for me to identify him with. A sure stamp that this was the man I was looking for.

Although my vision grew cloudy with tears, I could see enough to keep me awake for months, as it was the stuff of nightmares. His lips were fixed into a disturbing grimace, propped up by cotton wool which seemed to spill out from the corners of his mouth. His eyes were closed and sunken. Upon closer inspection, I could see staples peppering the back of his skull. I was immediately aware of the fact that he was much skinnier than when I'd last seen him. The deep scent of chemicals, which only just masked the unmistakable pungency of rot, filled my nostrils.

By now my grandfather was leaning into the makeshift bed, caressing my father's cold, frozen face and promising that he would look after me, whilst at the same time my other grandfather, my father's father, was wailing and crying for my father to wake up. It was quite the juxtaposition. My maternal grandfather stayed calm, telling the corpse of my dad that he wasn't to worry, his baby girl would not be alone. I gulped back the tears that had filled my eyes, afraid that if I really let go, I would drown us all in them, and we would soon be lying alongside him in our own adult Moses baskets. Instead, I leaned further in too, taking in all the loose hairs, the dry skin, the very fibres of the suit's fabric and breathing in the unbearable smell. I wanted to get as close as possible – not so much to this fading cocoon, but to death itself. I wanted so badly to see what was behind this cement veil. I wanted to dip my toe in morbid water just to see if understanding it all would make me feel better. My grandfather left me on my own; he could see it was important that I was able to have that final moment.

The rest of the day is a blur. It wasn't until I was writing this lesson, during Christmas 2020, that my grandfather reminded me of the fact that we had to jump the train barriers to get back home as neither of us had two pennies to rub together.

What I do remember is how the few weeks leading up

to the funeral were very chaotic for me. On the first evening of the Nine Night, I went to bed in the spare room in my father's house, a space in which I had slept perhaps over a hundred times before. I found myself wide awake. The fear consumed me. Being in his house and around all of his stuff – his trainers still in the position where he had kicked them off just before stepping into his study, his CDs strewn all around the living room, the Arsenal paraphernalia that seemed to pop up randomly throughout the house – was just too much. At 3am, I decided I couldn't take it any longer.

I got dressed and packed my pull trolley quickly. As I shoved the last bits inside, my eyes caught the cover of those cases they give you when you get passport photos. It was lying there on a shelf. Slowly, I opened it. There were two images of him. They were perhaps the last photos of him. Tenderly, I slid one of the images out of the puckered paper and stuffed it into my jeans pocket.

I tiptoed past his bedroom door. I knew there were relatives in it, and I didn't want them to hear me. As I slowly descended the stairs, I remembered the front door. There was always a bolt right at the top. I prayed that it was not locked. I had to go, now, and prising it open was going to make a lot of noise.

As I got closer, I realised my worst fears were confirmed. People were asleep nearby in the living room. I hesitated. But

I had to leave. Tentatively, I raised myself up. Stretching my upper body, I caught the bolt and rattled it until it moved.

'Clank,' it went.

I paused. There was a fleeting moment when part of me wanted to be caught, confronted, and then consoled. But when I realised no one had stirred, that moment passed, and I allowed myself to breathe again with relief. Gingerly, I picked up my trolley and opened the door, allowing the stiff cold air to freeze my tears.

The road was dark, and I was alone. On any other night I would have been concerned for my safety. But tonight, I feared for the person who would cross me. I felt like I had enough hate and anger in me to kill someone with my bare hands. I looked back at a house I instinctively knew I would never go back inside again. No one was coming to get me. I walked the half a mile to Blackhorse Road station, where I sat on my trolley and cried until the gates opened almost an hour later.

How different death and grief are.

Before my father died, I had experienced many interactions with death. I had stood in front of my great-grandmother's grave, which was covered with hot, sticky, pomegranate-coloured soil. I had kneeled behind rows of old Italian neighbours who had invited me to the sending off of their wonderful nonna, one half of a couple who had watched me grow up. I had seen the heavy tears of mothers who were reaching out for pews to be steadied, as the sadness of burying their sons, far earlier than they could have ever imagined, sought to pull them towards the floor. I had gasped at the news that a classmate had been stabbed to death and then reportedly raped as her blood gathered beneath her.

But all of those situations, those endings, as tragic as they were, had still allowed me to be just in the audience, to stand on the periphery, to get on with my life that had remained unchanged, unpunctured by personal heartache.

This was new to me. The grieving.

I saw my father everywhere: in his favourite songs, a film he liked, the latest Adidas trainers I am sure he would have loved. Worst still, even if I had been able to shut the world out, I only had to look in the mirror to see his face again. You know, sometimes I think God was on annual leave when it came to my creation and let his assistant do a quick copy and paste from my father. For years, I learned how to apply my make-up without making actual eye contact with myself. With him.

Sleep evaded me; I was too grief-stricken. I felt haunted. And truthfully, I have not slept soundly since he died. I often pretend that I'm a light sleeper due to the children, or I try to convince myself that it's how I've always been. But I can remember him barging into my room over the summer holidays because I would often sleep late into the afternoon.

'Jesus Christ, Cand!' He would laugh as he opened the blinds. 'Anyone would think you worked nights.'

For ages I dreamt of him. Sometimes in those dreams, I would reach out for him and he would pull me in for a hug so deep, I could feel the pulsating of his heart. I hated waking up. In the earlier months after he died, my one- or two-hour naps always had to be induced by alcohol. What little money I had was often used to facilitate my heavy drinking. A dark liquor of any kind would do. Tumbler after tumbler I'd drain, until my eyes could do nothing more but close themselves.

Grief turned me inside out. To this day, I often ask my therapist what God's purpose was in robbing me of my sensible, available, interested and supporting parent. Back then, on darker days which seemed to go on far too long, I often spoke aloud, questioning how he could leave me at the door of adulthood and expect me to do well. For years I blamed my nonchalance and self-sabotaging behaviour on his departure.

And for years I walked as if the world owed me something. I was so full of anger and sadness at the loss of one my most precious relationships. It physically hurt to act as if I were invested in cultivating another relationship of any kind. I was a biohazard, and became extremely comfortable with being confrontational. As far as I was concerned, I was the only person walking around with this kind of wound. No matter how far I walked and how long I searched, it was obvious that I would never find someone who would be able to understand me.

The way my father's death impacted on the family dynamics didn't help either. I don't know why, but I've noticed that in my community, grieving – a time reserved for sadness and soul-searching – can quickly become a slanging match. Using the excuse of shattered hearts, matured tensions can see families torn further apart rather than pulled closer together.

It didn't help that all the usual things, like personal artefacts or even a grave or knowledge of where my father's ashes were, weren't available to me. Yes, until this very day, I don't know where my father's remains are. The only people who ever seem shocked by that information are white folk. This isn't to say that the death of an important person doesn't rock their world, but there is an acute level of drama that can often come alongside grief that only my sistas can relate to.

As I got a little older, I realised that the disjointed, disrespectful and the determined disregard I was faced with when my father died was not a unique scenario. Although it wasn't quite a silver lining, it did feel comforting to know that I wasn't the only person living who felt like a castaway.

And to be honest, many of the tales I've heard have made my experience seem like a dream situation by comparison.

Whilst the Pisces in me seems to always return to its default setting, which is empathy, what I have been able to lean is this: just because someone hasn't experienced grief, or perhaps has reasons for shutting down their own grieving process, doesn't give them the right to dictate how another person should or shouldn't work their way through the dark tunnel of their own personal tragedy. As years went on and I felt myself feeling low or sad, especially around the anniversary of my dad's death, I was reminded how I had very obviously used up all my allotted down days.

'Child, you still ain't over that?'

The woman who asked was a family friend. One I would have usually been forced to call auntie or some shit. She was so nosy. She often popped in on her way home after checking on her food business. I was surprised she had any business at all because she clearly struggled to mind it, too busy was she gossiping and meddling in other people's affairs.

'Some things you just need to put to bed, you hear? Women of our kind don't have time for all of that. We are strong.'

She smiled, patting me on my shoulder as if we were close. She was right, I was strong, because I had successfully stopped myself from ramming her spectacles down her throat. She wasn't alone. It had become apparent that those closest to me expected me to just bury my feelings, like the ones we had lost. People die. Move on.

No one around me could empathise. My sole surviving parent still had both of hers. She tried to comfort me, but it was clear she was most confused by my deep desire to be held and understood. And another female in my life couldn't even muster the strength to pretend that she cared.

'You need to just get over it!' she yelled one day.

We were engaged in a face-off. I was heading out, and she stood blocking the front door.

'All of this crying!' she went on. 'He was never there for you anyway,' she lied.

'Get out of my way,' I growled, now seeing red instead of someone my community would have expected me to respect regardless of how they were treating me.

Before I could feel anything else, I felt the sting of a slap across my left cheek. Without thinking, I returned the favour and shoved her out of the way so that I could get out.

That was the common consensus, the idea that I was overdoing my grief. Surrounded by people who had not even begun to develop loving, mentoring, stable relationships with their now departed loved ones meant that this entire experience felt excruciatingly lonely. It also did not help that I was the only one in my current friendship group to suffer such a personal loss. No one knew what to do with me and for years I didn't know what to do with myself.

Over the years, I have found myself actively seeking out spaces where discussing grief and death are not frowned upon. Through things like podcasts, YouTube videos, books, and even online courses which help people unwrap their true feelings about death, I've been able to become part of a community who have learned to see no weakness in discussing how one can still be struggling two decades after the loss of a loved one. Because admittedly it got to the point where even I was exhausted by trying to fill this gaping void. How long can one cry? How long can one feel that no one understands them? The answer is: forever.

It is only very recently I heard someone say something which resonated deeply.

Your grief doesn't get any smaller, but your life gets bigger. Other things come in, good things – love, birth, welcome transformations – which take the edge off the pain. A pain that will always be there. One that I have even come to admire, as it is a representation of just how much my father meant to me. That deep longing, especially in times of adult crisis, is a reminder of just how positive an influence he was on my life.

Seeing as I lack material possessions of his and don't know of a headstone or a location where his ashes have been scattered, it was very important for me to develop rituals that could help offer me a similar solace as to what I imagine being able to tend to a physical grave must feel like. No matter where I've lived, I have needed to have a physical space for pictures, birthday cards, teddy bears and the like, which to me feels sacred. It's an altar of sorts, which encourages me to release sadness the moment I feel it stirring. One cannot underestimate the power of such a tangible thing.

Sometimes, when speaking to someone who has lost a loved one slowly and gradually, I often have to combat feelings of jealousy. I know. I feel most wretched for admitting that, but death came for my father so suddenly. I don't think it's just his giggle and soft grasp at the bottom of my neck that I miss; it is also the unanswered questions, it's the cold air in a space which could have perhaps been filled with last-minute requests or words of wisdom, even a knowing squeeze of the hand. This is of course a moot point, because whether we lose someone suddenly or over a longer period, all of us left here, on this side of the veil, wish we had had more time.

And that is one of the best lessons that losing someone so early could teach me: how clipped time is. You can hear a billion people say, 'life is short' in a million different variations, and like your first orgasm, learning to drive or even receiving your first payslip, you cannot possibly imagine the reality of such an experience until you've seen something for yourself. Looking over my dad's ashy cocoon, I remember being acutely aware of how ordinary this moment was once I disassociated myself. This is how it ends for everybody. Sure, the coffin may perhaps be more luxurious and the mortician may be a little more precise, but budget for such things aside, this end is something we all have in common. Having that experience so early on has really been the jump-start to me having my 'try it all' attitude.

But being open to most things isn't the only thing that this experience has given me. It's also made me very aware of how our continued practice of not saying how we feel can often have lifelong effects on those we leave behind.

'You know, I only thought about this today and it came up in therapy . . .' I paused, preparing myself for Bode's reaction. 'I can't be sure if my dad loved me.'

Bode immediately swung his eyes away from the television and stared at me. His response was measured.

'What are you saying?' he asked slowly, searching my features for any clues which could perhaps suggest this was some kind of joke.

'I know. But it feels good to say it. I cannot swear on the life of my kids that my dad loved me.' I was shocked at how unwavering my voice was.

'Woah. Where did this come from? From all I've heard

and read about your dad, I just don't see how you can come to that conclusion.'

Bode's tone was defensive now. It was cute watching him try to protect the memory of a man he had never met.

I looked down.

'I can't ever remember him saying it.' This time I whispered, not wanting the walls to hear me.

After a moment's silence, Bode just pulled me in for a hug.

It's true. I can remember his wide, determined, purposeful cursive. Birthday cards and the like signed 'Love, Dad.' But it's not quite the same thing as hearing it said to you.

His death inspired me to talk. To those who had been around me since birth, I assume they would say, I do far too much of it – the talking that is – as it perhaps reveals more about them, about us, than they would care to admit. But if I, his only child, couldn't even remember him saying he loved me, it made me question how much more he didn't say. I made a promise to myself that my children would never be able to ask the same questions of me.

As distant as I may appear to many others, I have a special softness and openness reserved for my children which I can only predict that they will soon find annoying. I tell them multiple times a day how much I love them. I smother them in kisses whilst they are doing nothing more than watching their favourite cartoons. If something or someone has upset me, I do not hide it from them. I am clear about who I think has their best interests at heart, and who does not. I am also very direct with my eldest about what I want to happen to my body should I unfortunately not be able to see them into adulthood. As morbid as it seems to others, including her father, nothing makes me prouder than Esmé discussing death as if it were no more than a trip to the dentist. Not welcomed, but necessary.

I think this sentence I've just written applies particularly well to this time in history we've all been living through. Many friends and colleagues were openly perturbed to find that Esmé perhaps knew more about Covid-19 and how deadly it was than they did. Evening after evening, she asked to sit with us as we watched a clearly nervous Prime Minister put forth a premature plan about how best to tackle this global pandemic.

'So, the death toll went up today?' she asked rhetorically after we all finished soaking in the latest statistics.

'Yeah,' I sighed. 'Does that scare you?' I asked, always willing to check that our liberal style of parenting is working for her too.

'Not really,' she mused. 'I mean, I don't want to die, but only because I will miss you. But we must die. Like your dad, you know?'

I could not help but crack a smile.

'I know,' I said, giggling.

Instead of being horrified, I'm pleased that Esmé is already comfortable talking about the inevitable. Whilst you cannot prepare yourself for the gut-wrenching grief that comes with losing a loved one, I think having clear discussions about what continues to be the biggest mystery to us mere mortals helps to set some ground rules for what to expect. We cannot avoid it. But we can be prepared, and give the younger ones in our lives the vocabulary to express how they feel about their own eventuality.

When writing my first book, I dedicated an entire chapter to the facts and my feelings surrounding knife crime in the UK, specifically London. I spent over seventy hours on Snapchat accounts and YouTube videos which unfortunately weren't that hard to find. Trying to understand the psyche of knife-wielding thirteen-year-olds led me to wondering how they seemed so unperturbed about taking someone's life, or risking their own.

'I would rather make a next man's mum cry, than see my mumsy cry innit,' one balaclava-wearing youth offered up. 'Death is just death innit. I don't fear dying at all. This is how it is out here. Live by the sword. Die by the sword.'

Instantly I felt overwhelmingly maternal and my instinct was to run my fingers along my laptop screen, tracing the outline of his body. Quite like his mother perhaps will when he does eventually end up dead. It was then I recognised that they do not fear death because it appears as though there is nothing to value in life. And that bit I understood. Ironically, death made me feel that way. After Dad died, I spent years questioning what the point of it all was, if this – that – is how we were all destined to finish up. Some endings are, unfairly, more brutal than others, but you are dead all the same.

After a decade of soul-searching, it became clear that the only difference is what we try to do with our time between the cradle and the grave. Because of the media and our obsession with celebrity, it seems as though our primary belief is that our offering, our time spent on this earth, has to be a constant explosion of fireworks: grand, full of colour and obvious to every passer-by. But I can attest that the people who have had the biggest impact on me weren't perhaps known by many at all, but their lives meant or still mean more than I can describe.

KJ died recently. Out of respect for their family, I will not go into details, but it's perhaps not an end any of us would wish for. Since my dad died, there have been more losses, but none of them affected me in the way that KJ's did. It feels as though along with themselves, a part of the true me decayed too.

Sitting on the edge of my bed the day of their funeral, I could not bring myself to go. So much had changed since we were fresh-faced teens in the BRIT School courtyard thinking the world was ours. And that's how I wanted to remember them. Losing Dad had taught me that I could stand at the side of their coffin until I myself became a corpse, but that spark was never going to return. As I slowly sent a text to a mutual friend, I allowed myself to unravel. Sliding to the floor and letting out a wail, it felt as if my body had been holding onto that for longer than I would care to admit. I hadn't felt that tug, the ferocity of that storm for an exceptionally long time. Once again, so many things had been left unsaid.

It was time to address this.

'So, Grandad, when you die, what should I do? Because listen, I'm not having another shitshow,' I warned, the second G&T making me feel bold enough to speak those words.

It was Christmas Eve. The children had long since gone to bed, buzzing with excitement at the thought of opening their gifts in the morning.

Bode gave my wrist a squeeze, as if to offer encouragement.

'Listen, I've got all the paperwork sorted and the funeral long paid for. You can come, but I will leave some money for you to have two bodyguards to protect you from—'

My laughter cut him off mid-sentence because I knew what he was about to say. The giggles helped alleviate some of the sadness surrounding what we were discussing.

'Grandad, I don't need you to pay for it,' I sighed.

'No, no, I'm not joking. You come with two bodyguards. The second you see that curtain drop, you get the fuck out of town. In and out, no bullshit, like the way I lived life. You come back home, fix a G&T, and get on with your life. Because where I'm going, they better have a pub.'

He smiled before sinking down his glass of whiskey.

'In all seriousness, you've delighted me, Boobie. It has been a pleasure to bring you so far. You have had your ups and downs, but my word, have you risen to the occasion. I told your father I would look after you and I know he would be so proud.'

His voice broke on the last word.

I felt hot tears streaming down my face. But they were not solely making an appearance because of what he'd just said, they were also cleansing. Here I was, finally learning from easily one of my life's hardest lessons. We need to ask each other what feel like difficult questions, now, without hesitation. Because the only burden heavier than the loss itself is the weight of wonder.

Some questions are more practical – I wonder if they would have preferred burial or cremation?

Some seemingly small – I wonder what flowers they would have liked?

But some will make you ponder forever – I wonder if they loved me?

And you know, I would not change a thing. I am incredibly grateful to grief and all of its teachings. It is a constant reminder to play to win. To show up with grace and try to do as well as I can. To not be afraid of stepping away from situations that no longer serve me. To change my mind, again and again. To try most things once, because at worst I might feel embarrassed, and at best, I come closer to creating a life which will make me greet death with open arms.

What I wish I'd known:

- I know they say time is a healer, but unfortunately there is no cut-off date for grieving. It comes in waves. It may perhaps never be as violent a storm as it was in the beginning, but over time you will gather resources to keep you dry on the rainy days that are yet to come.

- Speaking of resources, don't be afraid to seek out groups or tools that will help you manage the pain. Especially if you're part of a community that would rather not acknowledge the long-lasting effects of loss.

- If, like me, you are without somewhere to go to honour or 'be with' a deceased loved one, don't hesitate to put systems in place which can help resemble a place of rest.

- Don't be embarrassed to say you're afraid. Most of us fear the unknown, even if someone we still feel connected to has gone. A change in your sleeping pattern or feeling haunted is normal.

- Be selfish. Now is not the time to hold space for those who make a point of not understanding you.
- Bring death to the dinner table. Don't allow it to be a taboo subject. A moment of discomfort or dread is better than a lifetime of not knowing.

Lesson 10

CALL ME CUPID – ON SELF-LOVE

Love is not abusive.

Love is not based on circumstance.

Love is not convenient.

Love is not a barter.

Love is not a ration.

Love is not a reward.

Love is not coercive.

Love is not a tool.

Love is not a pause.

Love is not a ring.

These statements might sound obvious to some of you, but it has taken me a lifetime to begin to understand them. Learning what love is – and, maybe more importantly, what love isn't – has forced me to face up to the realisation that the pool of love available to me and the love I'm able to bestow on others hasn't always been as deep nor as wide as I would have liked. After a lot of reflection, I've had to sit with the fact that, for ages, I only really thought about love, loving and being loved in terms of being able to please someone else.

You see, for a long time, it seemed to me that I was only ever worth receiving love if the giver was pleased with how much I met their expectations. Most of my life, relationships seemed to only be loving if I was respectful and able to offer something, rather than anything more innate or instinctive. And this wasn't dissimilar for most of my friends. We cottoned on quickly that love was fleeting unless certain rules were abided by. It was always a barter. And love always seemed available if I was willing to provide something: emotional support, money, time, sex, lying, acceptance. You name it; I think I have traded it all for love.

It felt like, for many of those around me, love was low down on the list of requirements and could be turned on and off like a switch, depending on the mood of the person controlling that switch. This means I did not hear 'I love you' very often. Those words were missing from almost everyone's vocabulary, even my father's, as I pointed out to Bode that evening. Instead, they were replaced – and still are – with phrases such as: 'Look how much I've done for you!', and 'I don't need to tell you I love you – you should know.'

To me, it felt as if there was only one person whose love was not conditional on me being appealing or appeasing.

'Girl, you know Grandad loves you without hiccup,' my maternal grandfather would say, pulling me in for a hug so tight that his layered woody scent of pipe residue would go straight to my head.

Knowing that my grandfather loved me in the purest way made all the difference when it came to me fighting to share that feeling with someone else, regardless of how many times my own heart had been broken. I knew what was missing. It was life-changing to see through example that love is not only a verb, it is also a noun. Not only would my grandad say he loved me, but he understood the value placed upon doing so.

Love was packing up cardboard boxes with necessities like sugar, flour, bread and milk and handing them over, not knowing how he would eat himself.

Love was visiting me in a hostel begging me to wean myself off drugs, and not judging me for the life I was living at the time.

Love was providing me with books even though he himself could not read.

Love was a constant desire to surrender his own coat in order to protect me from the harsh storms life brought, even if his own umbrella was broken.

Love was leaning over my father's dead body, kissing his

forehead and telling him that his baby girl would never be alone.

Only now am I beginning to deal with the kind of grief that comes with suspecting that, from my perspective, the love I have craved will never be, apart from my grandfather. This lesson has come at a cost so large that for years, I refused to cough up. I was always willing to bend, change, expand and contract if only to feel loved for a few moments. Being so willing to compromise only seemed to attract people who wanted to bathe in the warmth of being loved rather than loving me back, which only warped my understanding of it even further. For too long, all I ever thought love was – the only one worth looking for and compromising myself for – was the love that a man could bestow upon me. But as time has moved on and I have sought to educate myself, it has become apparent that there are many more versions of love beyond my old narrow ideas, and in my opinion they should be just as – if not, in many cases, more – important than the love we are told we can find in a partner.

As I wrote about in Lesson 2, there is love that one can only find in true friendship – connections that seem to remain in place no matter what life throws in our way. I have found that this kind of love is the medicine for romantic heartbreaks, job losses, miscommunications within family structures and more. This can be the best kind of love of all.

Like a roaring fire, it must be stoked and kept an eye on, but with the right attention, it's the kind of love that can last a lifetime.

There is the love that usually exists between parent and child. Of course, I wanted to write '*mother* and child', but the reality is that there are some mothers who do not love their children, just as there are some fathers who take on the role of primary caregiver who are more present than not. Those fathers are often written out of the loving narrative, because from conception to cradle and beyond, it's usually the mother who gets first dibs on what parental love signifies. When things flow as we hope they should, the love from parent to child and back helps to raise people who are lucky enough to have a clear understanding of what love is and what it is not. As a parent myself – of children I hope already know how much I love them – I have come to discover that the love I have for them trumps all else. It even comes before the love I have for the man who went halves on creating them. Through this version of love, I am constantly tested and educated in selflessness, in what it means to love another without expectations, and about loving another even when they trigger feelings which are usually labelled as disappointment or shame.

Then, of course, there is self-love. This is the one I struggle with the most, perhaps because it's the one I know the least about. Whilst my love for certain friends, my children and my significant other never seem to waiver, I can chart exactly when and how I seem unable to love myself. The reason these times are obvious for me is because the moments in my life where I most struggled with self-love are also the times I felt my life was hanging off the edge of the cliff. The times when I have felt the most troubled, unsure, and out of whack are all in alignment with when I loved myself the least. That's why I find it hard to agree with the idea that, in order to practise other versions of love, you must declare yourself the undisputed champion of loving oneself. Through experience, I have learned that my inability to top up on self-love is sometimes because I have overspent my reserves on loving others who perhaps didn't deserve it. But more of that a little down the line.

In my opinion, self-love is ever-mutating. I think the best thing one can do is work on the roots and accept that the more visible elements – the leaves, flowers, stems – will always be changing. That's why self-love is much more than standing naked in front of the mirror and reciting affirmations (although that helps). It is also more than sharing images of yourself from an unflattering angle and trying to encourage others to love themselves (although that helps too). I think self-love is about being able to say out loud things about yourself that you fear could make another person fall out of love with you. When you're on that precipice between stagnation and freedom, self-love can help you move closer to the latter. A landscape of carnage can start looking like a field of flowers once you love yourself more than you fear losing the love of someone else.

Self-love has no regard for public adoration. It does not work like that. Self-love and the constant review of it is deeply personal, which is why it's usually not those who are the quickest to publicly proclaim how much they love themselves who are the best at actually doing so. I know this to be true, as I have been that person many times. Feeling desperately unloved and filled with self-hate, I found the quickest way to camouflage these feelings was to prove to everyone else that I really, really loved myself – from half-naked selfies to conversations with friends where I tried to come across as a wisdom-filled preacher. All of those things were a smoke-screen.

In the absence of self-love, I have, like many others, tried to fool myself that the love of another should surely be able to plug that gap, if only intermittently. For a myriad of reasons, I genuinely believed that love, specifically romantic love, was never available to me. This belief was strengthened by never seeing women like myself loved. In sitcoms, women like me were never the popular students nor the quirky girls next door; never the ones getting married nor the ones whose hearts were broken. Love was not available by existence nor example. As previously discussed, I am not unaware of the struggles many women who share my hue are still faced with in this day and age. Social media especially operates like a snow globe. No matter how hard I shake, the scene remains the same: black women bearing the brunt of disregard, disrespect and distaste. I see the younger black women around me, at first youthful and full of fight, defending their right to be loved, expressing their dismay at constantly being deemed as unloveable, even from those who they feel deeply connected to. And then they get weary, and find other ways to heal their hearts, until the natural rallying cry for love turns to a scream full of spite directed at love in any form at all.

Not everyone is going to love you – that much is a fact. But, because I wasn't good at self-love, I couldn't hack it whenever I was rejected. Instead, like I said, I decided to double-down on pleasing and loving others, hoping that the fact I was making these men feel good about themselves would mean that I would be worthy of their validation, attention and, in due course, a slice of their love. Sis, I was realistic enough to understand that loving someone like me with all their heart would be a godlike task for most men, so I always told myself that something was better than nothing; that I needed to remain grateful that someone dared to love me at all. But, even with that in mind, for me it was never enough. Even when a suitor was only too happy to give me a portion of the love I required, my heart would become greedy. Insatiable, even. And as they became more and more used to my pleasing them, and their demands for more attention, ego-boosting and support ever increased, their love for me in turn dwindled. As time passed, my heart hardened, and I was able to convince myself that perhaps I did not require love at all.

We all require love. But I didn't know that at the time. And in not knowing that vital truth, I tried to fix the game so I wouldn't have to muster the strength to try and catch someone's heart once more. My mantras changed to:

Me against the world.

Catch flights not feelings.

Felwed out not fucked over.

Play with people so they do not end up playing with you.

Born alone, die alone.

Trust no one. Especially not no man.

Yadda, yadda, yadda.

I became obsessed with appearing allergic to even the thought of being in love, being loved and giving my love to someone else. Describing love as the ultimate deal-breaker became a regular thing for me to do.

Now I'm a little surer of myself, I can readily admit that my cocky comebacks designed to show the outside world that I thought love was a wet and unnecessary accessory to a proudly independent life were not genuine. What I was really saying was: someone, please love me.

And when the time came, when the first scent of love in the shape of Bode did begin to penetrate the atmosphere, at first I wrote it off as eau de toilette instead of parfum. Like jewels I thought were fake, I was expecting the equivalent of a rash to spread across my neck and, like a well-trained dealer, I tested the gem's purity constantly. This . . . love, the love I had so often downplayed because it couldn't possibly be genuine in my opinion – I had to keep an eye on it.

'So, what's the catch?' I would wonder aloud, circling this love like a panther waiting to lash out at any moment.

It didn't help that, as ever, all around me I was flooded with the reality of everyone else's lack of faith. It made me a firm non-believer. What encouraged me further to grind my heels in and stay committed to the idea that this display of love was nothing but a ruse, a way to open my heart so I could be led down a garden path, was that Bode had fallen in love with me before I had the chance to fall in love with myself. I was riddled with self-doubt. Surely his love for me was meaningless, I'd tell myself, because I didn't have a deep enough love for myself. I found the concept of love without judgement to be untrustworthy, because for as long as I had been able to put my nose into grown-up people's business, the common consensus was that love was a fallacy.

'You stay there, all that love shit will leave you fucked over.'

'Since I got divorced, I decided to never make the mistake of falling in love again. You better mind yourself.'

'Sis, I don't think my own mother has the capacity to love me. So, these boys? Nah, they could never.'

No one genuinely loved you and you sure as hell shouldn't truly love them. Even when it came to the person you shared your bed with, you'd never be able to relax because at any moment they would reveal to you that, in fact, they never really loved you at all. It was an exhausting way to live life.

As I have allowed myself to soften and believe that I am capable of loving others as well as myself, I am starting to see how sad it was that I never entertained the idea of true love at all. I continued to block myself off from love. To say that the market for love was oversaturated. To claim that those who allowed themselves to open up to love were destined for failure.

I was berating the thing I thought I couldn't be. You know, like how we reason with ourselves that the person we have never met must be a bitch because they seem to have everything we think we can never attain? Yeah, that.

But there are no miracles here. Just because I'm coming

around to these ideas and now know that the love on offer is genuine, it doesn't mean I don't sway or feel deeply uncomfortable when I'm caught off-guard. It's usually my friends who highlight how far I have to go. After a catch-up about work and our children, or following idle gossip, one friend will always say, 'I love you so much!' as we close the call. The first time it tumbled from her mouth, I had to physically clutch my chest as if doing so would help control my emotional reaction to this unprompted declaration. I couldn't speak. The first time, I thought it might be a one-off thing, said quickly and without thinking. But she kept at it, seemingly unperturbed by my unwillingness to offer her a response.

Silently, I had to unpack my immediate throat closure. It took not even an hour to realise that her words had unearthed those early fears and falsehoods. The ones that said I was unloveable, that love doesn't come without a condition, that love is not free. The ones that said that love was rooted in distrust. I had to fight with those memories to convince myself that she really did think I was special. I had to physically make a list of all the ways she had shown me she loved me. The way she had shown up and out for nothing in return, nothing at all. Through doing so, I also realised that I loved her too. I imagined her not being in my life and I at once became depressed and grumpy, even though the mere thought was all pretend. I thought about how, should anything happen to her children, I would pick up whatever and wherever. It was love, alright. I loved her too.

And so, with much work, I responded to her openness. I am still training myself to believe that there is no cap on how much love one can receive, nor is there a need to constantly weigh up whose love is truer. I am starting to trust love when I see it. Getting to this point in one very short lifetime has been one of my greatest personal fights, although I'll be the first to admit that just because I am learning that I am loved, that doesn't make me a gold medallist in self-love. I have resigned myself to the fact that living without affliction may always be a struggle.

And then there is parental love, which is something so grand, I often struggle to communicate its depth. Strangely, for me it is one of the versions of love that overrules the idea of love at first sight. Because before I was able to decipher if the motions that stirred within me were the movements of a baby or trapped wind, I loved my children far more than I have ever loved anyone else.

And now they are here, I am resolute.

I tell everyone (and God forbid this be a tempt of fate) that, should my children be the perpetrator of something heinous – and I don't mean where they dare to antagonise someone's morals, but where they take part in the sort of crime I cannot bring myself to describe – I will continue to publicly love them. In the house, I might break things and wail and wonder if my womb was cursed, but from the cradle to the grave I will remain committed to loving them. Because that is what being loved has taught me. It must extend past the unthinkable. Because if it doesn't, is it really love at all?

Loving them has helped me to recognise and reconcile with the past me, who has done all sorts in the hope it would lead to love. Loving a child has forced me to reach back and offer my ashy-kneed, Afro-wearing, thick-glasses-sporting, childlike self a hug and more. That for me was a necessity. Because she was still waiting.

Excuse me, correction, she is still waiting.

It's perhaps why now my children tire of my made-up songs, in which the lyrics are nothing but out of tune 'I love you's on repeat. Or maybe it's why I drive myself crazy trying to be at every assembly, pack every lunch and feign interest in every piece of school artwork.

'You're going to drive yourself mad,' Bode tells me.

I shrug, very aware of how he cannot possibly understand what I am trying to give them, and why I am doing this.

When it comes to love, I know I am first in line to end some deep-seated generational curses. This pile-on of conditional love and lack of warmth stops with me because I know only too well what can happen in one's life when lovelessness is not confronted. I cannot entertain it for my children. I need them to know. I want you to know. Hell, I need to know.

We need to always look and reach back to the parts of ourselves that still feel that they aren't worthy of being loved.

You were worthy of love as a child.

You are worthy of love as an adult.

You are worthy of love, period.

My dear, you are.

And I'm not saying that to make you feel like you're being pulled in for a bear-hug by a larger-chested lady who smells of Werther's Originals whilst slipping you a tenner when no one is looking. Then again, if that's how it comes across, I don't apologise for it. I have waited an awfully long time to have an abundance of that feeling: to be so loved, no matter what, that I am just waiting to give some of my excess to those that are not so topped up. This does not mean that I have a perfect understanding of love or that I am unaware of how, sometimes, love is one-sided, unfair, or used as tool of distraction – or worse still, a weapon – in the wrong hands. All those things are true too.

But what is also true is that love, of all kinds, can be so sweet and thirst-quenching that you will not only repeatedly want to drink from its well, you will also be intent on sharing it. I hope you accept my offer.

What I wish I'd known:

- Self-love is a lifelong journey.
- The love of a significant other is not the be-all and end-all when it comes to love.
- Whilst empathy is wonderful, you don't have to wait for people to learn how to love you.
- Loving is just as important as being loved.
- There is no stand-in for love.

THE MOST IMPORTANT LESSON OF ALL

When the question 'Would you prefer to be liked or respected?' used to arise, I have to acknowledge that my younger self would always choose to be liked. Because I did not yet understand that being liked is usually about pleasing others and being respected is a result of pleasing oneself. So if you take nothing else from what I've learned thus far, please remember to always please yourself.

ACKNOWLEDGEMENTS

As ever, first and continued thanks to the Most High.

Secondly, Candice, sis, you did it again, girl. I really rate you. It wasn't easy, but you got it done. I hope this process has taught you how important it is to slip off your superwoman cape and delegate. The empire, as you can already see, is going to need more faithful hands to help build it. Let them in.

Dad, book two, can you believe it? Heavenly drinks on me as soon as I touch down.

Grandad, thank you for always reminding me to seek guidance, wisdom and understanding.

Papa B, I love you.

Esmé-Olivia, my true hope is that you are able to use this book as a lamp unto your feet as you grow older and wiser. Being a mother to you is a true privilege.

RJ, you're still a little too young for this kind of book, but I hope that by the time you are able to read it, the information will help you be a better brother to your sisters and brotha to your sistas.

To my family, who include, but aren't limited to, Remi Sadé, Karlene Norman, Leona Satchell-Samuels, Emma Fowler, Francesca Zampi, Shamara Speed, Ngoni Chikwenengere, Mahlon Evans-Sinclair, Angel Dee and Helen Beany. I would exceed the word count if I were to truly express how much your support as individuals and a community means to me and my family. I love you all.

Krish, I saw a picture of you the other day and I couldn't help but smile. Whilst my heart is on the heavier side due to your transition to the heavenly kingdom, I also know that wallowing is not an option. Nails on fleek, always.

Leeanne Adu, let's be honest, this book perhaps would not have gone to print on time if it wasn't for you. Thank you for joining our team and tightening up the ship.

To the entire team at Found Entertainment, we did it again, baby. Thank you for being just as ready to batten down the hatches as you are to pop champagne.

Thank you to the entire team at Quercus, but extra special thanks to Katy Follain, Bethan Ferguson, Elizabeth Masters and Ana McLaughlin.

And finally, to you, the reader. Be you a sista, sister or even a brother, thank you for staying until the very end.

Until next time,

Stay blessed.

Cx